www.AccuBiz.net
We're In Business To Help Your Business Succeed

www.AuraWealth.com
Helping Individuals Make Work Optional

1301 Southwest Blvd
Jefferson City MO 65109
Phone: (573) 634-4006
Fax: (573) 634-TAXX(8299)
Email: contact@accubiz.net

"We would like to offer this complimentary book to help promote your success and let you know we are available to help in that journey."

Six Steps to Small Business Success

Start, Manage, and Exit Your Business: 5 CPAs on Entrepreneurship

Bert Doerhoff, CPA;
Lowell Lillge, CPA;
David Lucier, CPA;
R. Sean Manning, CPA;
and
C. Gregory Orcutt, CPA

A Product of Biz Books, LLC

iUniverse, Inc.
Bloomington

Six Steps to Small Business Success
Start, Manage, and Exit Your Business:
5 CPAs on Entrepreneurship

Copyright © 2011 by Biz Books, LLC
Bert Doerhoff, CPA; Lowell Lillge, CPA; David Lucier, CPA;
R. Sean Manning, CPA; and C. Gregory Orcutt, CPA

All rights reserved. No part of this book may be used or reproduced by any means, graphic, electronic, or mechanical, including photocopying, recording, taping or by any information storage retrieval system without the written permission of the publisher except in the case of brief quotations embodied in critical articles and reviews. The views expressed in this work are solely those of the author and do not necessarily reflect the views of the publisher, and the publisher hereby disclaims any responsibility for them.

Product names, logos, brands, and other trademarks featured or referred to herein are the property of their respective trademark holders. These trademark holders are not affiliated with this publication. They do not sponsor or endorse our publication.

The material provided herein is for informational purposes only and is not legal advice either expressed or implied. You should contact your attorney to obtain advice with respect to any particular issue or problem.

The material provided herein is for informational purposes only and does not represent tax advice either expressed or implied. You should seek professional tax advice for tax questions and assistance. To ensure compliance with IRS Circular 230, any U.S. federal tax advice provided herein is not intended or written to be used, and it cannot be used by the recipient or any other taxpayer (i) for the purpose of avoiding tax penalties that may be imposed on the recipient or any other taxpayer, or (ii) in promoting, marketing or recommending to another party a partnership or other entity, investment plan, arrangement or other transaction addressed herein.

Strategic Coach®, Unique Ability®, and Unique Ability® Activities are registered trademarks, protected by copyright and integral concepts of The Strategic Coach Inc. All rights reserved. Used with written permission. www.strategiccoach.com

The Referability Habits™ is a trademark, protected by copyright and an integral concept of The Strategic Coach, Inc. All rights reserved. Used with written permission.

iUniverse books may be ordered through booksellers or by contacting:

iUniverse
1663 Liberty Drive
Bloomington, IN 47403
www.iuniverse.com
1-800-Authors (1-800-288-4677)

Because of the dynamic nature of the Internet, any web addresses or links contained in this book may have changed since publication and may no longer be valid.

Any people depicted in stock imagery provided by Thinkstock are models, and such images are being used for illustrative purposes only. Certain stock imagery © Thinkstock.

ISBN: 978-1-4620-0999-2 (sc)
ISBN: 978-1-4620-1000-4 (e)

Printed in the United States of America
iUniverse rev. date: 10/26/2011

CONTENTS

Author Acknowledgements ix

Introduction xiii

Before You Read This Book xix

Step 1.   Pre-Business Planning 1

Chapter 1.   The Dream: Running Your Own Business with Integrity 3

Chapter 2.   Pick the Right Business for You 9

Chapter 3.   Self-Evaluation for Small-Business Success . . . 15

Chapter 4.   Advisers for Your Business 19

Chapter 5.   Buying a Franchise or Starting from the Ground Up 25

Chapter 6.   The Business Plan: Creating the Map to Your Success 29

Chapter 7.   Strategic Marketing Planning 35

Chapter 8.   Partnerships and Agreements for Multiple Owners 43

Chapter 9.   Business Format and Tax Structure 47

Chapter 10.   Business, Family, and Personal Relationships: Making Them Work 55

Step 2.   Start-Up: Finances, Budgets, and Numbers . . . 59

Chapter 11.   Business Loans: A General Overview 61

Chapter 12.   Another Use for Your Business Plan 71

Chapter 13.	How to Read Financial Statements 75
Chapter 14.	Key Operating Statistics (Vitals) 83
Chapter 15.	Key Operating Statistics (Vitals) Comparison to Industry Standards 89
Chapter 16.	Tax Planning 93
Chapter 17.	Real Estate and Your Business 99
Chapter 18.	Insurance: A General Overview 103

Step 3.	Human Resources: The People Factor 109
Chapter 19.	Assembling Your Team 111
Chapter 20.	Compensation and Benefits 121
Chapter 21.	Training Employees 125
Chapter 22.	Managing Staff 129
Chapter 23.	Terminating Staff 135

Step 4.	Operations: Work Flow, Customers, and Sales . . 143
Chapter 24.	Managing Daily Operations 145
Chapter 25.	Managing Customers: Credit, Collections, and Service 151
Chapter 26.	Managing Marketing and Sales: Some Low-Cost Tips 157
Chapter 27.	Managing Growth and Expansion 169

Step 5.	Building a Salable Business and the Sale 173
Chapter 28.	Is It Time to Sell? 175
Chapter 29.	Selling and Valuing Your Business 179
Chapter 30.	Tax Planning for the Sale 185
Chapter 31.	Who Are the Buyers? 189
Chapter 32.	Negotiating the Sale 195

Chapter 33.	Sale Documents and Escrows for Contingencies	201
Chapter 34.	Transitioning Customers and Employees through the Sale	209
Step 6.	**Transitioning to Life after Business**	**215**
Chapter 35.	Life after Business: Wealth Management and Investments	217
Chapter 36.	Life after Business: Lifestyle Changes	227
Chapter 37.	Life after Business: Leaving a Legacy of Values	231

Glossary 239

Further Reading 243

Recommended Websites: 247

Bibliography 249

Author Acknowledgements

We would first like to extend our deepest gratitude to our families who have allowed us to dream big and have supported us from the beginning. We would not be who we are today if not for our parents, wives and children.

We also want to thank our teams of employees who have allowed us to create the businesses we have today. Without their dedication to serving our clients we would not have the experiences we write about in this book.

Forward
PASBA

The five authors of this book were brought together when we joined a nationwide network called the Professional Association of Small Business Accountants (PASBA). PASBA members are some of the best and brightest small business accounting, payroll, tax, and business advisory experts in the country, with one goal in mind – your small business success.

The unique collaboration of five CPA's was the brain child of one of our authors, Greg Orcutt, CPA, who came up with the idea at one of PASBA's semi-annual national conferences. We have all been members of PASBA for many years and three of us have been presidents of the organization. PASBA has helped us change our firms to allow us to deliver the absolute best service to small businesses. We are deeply indebted and grateful to all the PASBA members and want to personally thank each and every one of them.

PASBA is found at SmallBizAccountants.com

Special Recognition

Dr. Stephen E. Haag Ph.D.

The authors would also like to give a special thanks and recognition to Dr. Stephen E. Haag Ph.D.

Steve volunteered his time to read and critique early drafts of this book. As a result the authors were able to use Steve's recommendations to update not only the book's contents, but he also played a key role in how the book was formed into steps and assisted in providing a logical sequence to the chapters. Steve is a university teacher, dedicated educator, community volunteer and author himself; a true spirit behind the book. We are all greatly appreciative of Steve's direction and coaching which allowed us to compile our experience, training and thoughts into this book, *Six Steps to Small Business Success*.

Introduction

This book is written by five CPAs with a combined experience of one hundred-plus years in operating their own businesses and assisting thousands of other business owners in starting, managing, owning, buying, and selling businesses. Each CPA wrote separate chapters in the book depending on his areas of expertise, so you will notice slight changes in writing style as you move throughout the book.

There are so many things you never learn in a classroom. This book summarizes the lessons learned in the classroom of life, where mistakes can mean the difference between success and failure. Many entrepreneurs fail, not because they have a bad idea, but rather because they don't have the knowledge and skills it takes to convert their ideas into success. You might say that this book is a series of simple steps or ideas that business owners should find useful as they work to convert their dreams into reality.

As you read the brief biography below of the five authors, you will notice something unique. They all have strong experiences and professional accomplishments. However, it is their commitment to the future through their service to education, civic duties, charity, and family that makes them great business advisers. Bert Doerhoff has a saying: "Don't tell me how much you know until you show me how much you care." The authors have the knowledge, but their success is a direct result of how much they care about their clients and others.

Bert Doerhoff, CPA

After working for an international CPA firm, Bert thought he knew it all, so he moved a thousand miles back home and started his own CPA firm from scratch in 1978. Those first years were brutal, but he learned from his mistakes and the firm was later named one of the top fifty most innovative firms in the nation. Since then he has been featured and quoted in various national publications. Over the years he started separate firms to better serve clients in the areas of wealth management and payroll. Bert says, "I always strive to hire those who care about others and are smarter than I am, because I can learn from them and I want our clients to have the very best."

In addition to professional accomplishments, he has served on various civic, religious, and charitable boards with a special emphasis on training the leaders of tomorrow. He was elected president of the Missouri Association of Rural Education and still serves on the local public school board. Having raised four children, Bert offers one last piece of advice: "Anyone who thinks they have all the answers should just raise another child."

David J. Lucier, CPA

David is an entrepreneur, real estate investor, certified public accountant (CPA), and business adviser. He has worked with hundreds of start-up and emerging companies over the past thirty years. His management advice encompasses strategy, marketing, sales, finance, and operations.

He has served as a board member on numerous nonprofit organizations and has received various awards, including the prestigious U.S. Small Business Administration's "Accountant Advocate of the Year." He is also widely regarded as the top business lecturer in Rhode Island.

Lowell G. Lillge, CPA

Lowell received his accounting degree from the University of Wisconsin–Whitewater, where he also received his commission in the U.S. Army as a Second Lieutenant. He served six years in the U.S. Army Reserve while working at the world headquarters of Sentry® Insurance. When Lowell left Sentry® Insurance in 1983, he started his own accounting firm, specializing in bookkeeping, accounting, tax preparation and counseling, and payroll check-writing services for small businesses in the southeast Wisconsin area. He has held various offices (president, secretary, treasurer, and board member) in national and local professional associations. Lowell has worked with hundreds of clients over the years. One of his greatest joys is to watch his clients grow to meet their goals and even exceed them.

Lowell has been happily married to Sue since 1974. She has worked with him since the inception of the accounting practice. They have two children: Kristen is married and teaching in Iola, Wisconsin; Nathan is married and working with the Sacramento Regional Conservation Corps.

R. Sean Manning, CPA

Sean has over twenty years experience in the tax, accounting, and business consulting profession. He has a Bachelor of Science in Restaurant Management, and in 1995 he became a CPA after studying accounting. Sean has owned several different businesses and is currently an owner of or an investor in four different businesses. These and several other business endeavors round out Sean's business and professional experiences. He is a real estate owner and consultant to business owners. He also volunteers hundreds of hours a year supporting the business community and does public speaking on numerous business-related topics. Much of Sean's experience comes from his CPA firm, Manning & Company, PC™, which has a full-time staff supporting hundreds of businesses and business owners with valuable monthly financial information and advice. He supports business owners by defining and meeting their goals, evaluating growth opportunities, building a tax plan that can be executed, and providing guidance toward a successful transition of their business. In 2008, PASBA named Manning & Company, PC, "Innovative Accounting Firm of the Year" for its use of Web-based software solutions and paperless systems. Sean also enjoys many outside activities with family and friends in his home state of Colorado. Most enjoyable are skiing in the winter and golf in the summer with his wife Marilyn and two sons Chandler and Ethan.

C. Gregory Orcutt, CPA
Greg has over twenty-five years of experience helping businesses and individuals meet their financial goals. He has a Bachelor of Science in Accounting from Elmhurst College and an MBA from Xavier University. Greg has worked with very large companies since he started his career in a "Big Eight" accounting firm in Chicago. He now works with smaller companies in his business, Orcutt & Company, CPAs, in the greater Cincinnati, Ohio, area. He has served in various leadership positions in local professional and charitable organizations. "I love running and growing a business and helping my clients do the same. But nothing compares to the joy of raising our four children with my wife, Karen, and seeing them pursue their God-given purpose."

In 2008, he received the "Small Firm of the Year" award from the Professional Association of Small Business Accountants (PASBA). Greg enjoys the challenge of growing his business but also likes to travel and spend time with family.

Now you know the authors and why they wrote the book. Let's take a look at how the book is laid out.

The book is divided into six main sections:

1. **Pre-Business Planning:** Planning for the life cycle of a small business
2. **Start-Up: Finances, Budgets, and Numbers:** What you and your banker need to get started

3. **Human Resources: The People Factor:** Managing people
4. **Operations: Work Flow, Customers, and Sales:** Managing your office
5. **Building a Salable Business and the Sale:** Preparing the business for transition and sale
6. **Transitioning to Life after Business:** Helping the owner transition to life after the sale and legacy issues

The unique thing about the six steps of the book is that you can start anywhere in the book depending on where you are in the life of your business. Take a minute to read the next section and you can self-test to see what area of the book you want to read first.

Before You Read This Book

We intentionally designed this book so that you can jump in and start with the chapter that fits where your business is today. Whether you're just developing a business idea or you're looking to sell your ongoing enterprise, the sections of the book can be used as you see fit.

Of course, we think everyone can probably gain from reading the whole book, because there are lots of golden nuggets throughout. However, to get the most immediate impact, you might want to ask yourself the following questions to get a sense of where you may need the most help. In general, your answer to the questions will help you determine the steps and chapters of the book that may be of most interest to you. For example, what consumes the most of your time in your current business? Is it managing employees, trying to grow sales, or putting out day-to-day fires? If you decide employees are your biggest problems, then skip to Step 3 on human resources to get some immediate relief. Then you can go back and pick up on other key areas. Now let's look at the six key steps of the book and examples of day-to-day questions that each step will address.

Step 1: Pre-Business Planning

First, there is the excitement of all the planning that goes into starting your own business. A little planning on the front end goes a long way to ensuring the dream you pictured becomes a reality. Many businesses fail because the entrepreneur is a good technician at producing a particular business service or good but not necessarily a good businessperson. So if you are starting a new business, take a few minutes and learn from the experiences of others who have succeeded there. Section 1 will help you answer these questions:

- Do you know what type of business or service best fits your dream?
- Have you selected the right business for you?
- Have you evaluated yourself for small-business success?
- Do you have the right form of doing business (corporation, sole proprietorship, etc.)?
- Do you have the right advisers supporting you?
- Should you look at a franchise, buy another business, or start from scratch?
- Do you have a business plan in place?
- Do you have a strategic marketing plan in place?
- Do you have the correct partnership agreements in place for multiple owners?
- Do you have the right tax structure for your business to minimize income taxes?
- How do you coordinate business and family life?

Step 2: Start-Up: Finances, Budgets, and Numbers

Once you start the business, there are certain key fundamentals and tracking mechanisms you must put in place to keep things on track and grow the business. Business success is a constantly moving target, so you have to take the time to learn what your tracking mechanisms and your customers are telling you. Section 2 will help you answer these questions:

- Do you have the right type of financing and business loans?
- Do you know how to read financial statements and understand what they can tell you about your business?
- Do you know what the key operating statistics are for your business?
- Do you know how you compare to industry standards?
- Do you know what your tax liability will be for the current year?
- Have you considered your options for commercial real estate?
- Do you have the right insurance coverage?

Step 3: Human Resources: The People Factor
Hiring, training, and firing employees are all necessary parts of running a business. Section 3 will help you answer these questions:

- How do you go about hiring, interviewing, and screening employees?
- Are you paying a fair wage and competitive benefits?
- How are you training your new employees?
- Are you managing staff effectively?
- Do you know the right way to terminate an employee to protect yourself?

Step 4: Operations: Work Flow, Customers, and Sales
Daily operations involve numerous decisions about your product, service, and customers. Section 4 will help you answer these questions:

- Do you have systems in place so that your product or service is consistent?
- How do you manage your customers, grant credit, and respond to customer service issues?

- Do you have a sales and marketing plan in place, and do you adjust for market changes?
- Do you know when to expand your business?

Step 5: Building a Salable Business and the Sale

Once you have the business running smoothly, you need to plan for the eventual sale. Growing that saleable business takes some planning. Then once you decide to sell the business, there is a whole new set of issues: What is it worth? How do I transfer the customers to the buyer? What about the employees? How do I negotiate the terms of the sale? Section 5 will help you answer these questions:

- Does your business run smoothly without you?
- What is your business worth?
- Have you managed your debt so that you can afford to sell your business?
- How can you minimize the tax consequences of a sale?
- Who are the buyers for your business?
- What do you need to know to negotiate a sale contract, and who should be involved?
- How do you transition your customers to a new owner of your business?
- How do you transition your employees to a new owner of your business?
- What should you expect in the sale documents, and how will you structure the monetary transaction?

Step 6: Transitioning to Life after Business

Once you've made the decision to sell, how do you manage the transition for everyone involved? How will you adjust to your life after the business? Section 6 will help you answer these questions:

- What do you need to know about wealth management?
- How do you adjust to life after work?

- How do you pass on your values to your kids?
- How do you leave a legacy after you are gone?

Now pick the area that will have the most immediate impact for you, and start reading.

One last thought: Dream big, but always break it down into small steps, because small steps are easy to achieve and a lot of small steps equal one big step and a lot of big steps equal your dream.

STEP 1:

PRE-BUSINESS PLANNING

Chapter 1

The Dream: Running Your Own Business with Integrity

By Bert Doerhoff, CPA

In the introduction, we ended with a statement about your dreams and how you achieve them one small step at a time. This book is all about the decision processes needed to transition through the whole business life cycle from start-up to life after the business.

This chapter is about laying out a plan for your dreams and understanding the morals, ethics, and responsibilities you will need in order to achieve those dreams—by taking steps. In order to successfully achieve all these various steps, there is a common theme that must run throughout your business, and that theme is integrity.

The Dream

When you build something, before you start a project you have a picture in your mind of what the end product should look like and the benefits you will derive from it. Business and life are no different, but most of us ignore that very simple concept. We all should spend some time planning our business and personal lives and decide what our dream of success and wealth really looks like.

It is like running a race and not knowing when you reach the finish line. How exciting is that? Over the years I have noticed that the 10 percent of the population who set goals for themselves out achieve the 90 percent who don't. Therefore, the very first thing you should do is decide what your dream and goals are.

Once you have the dream, the next step is to break it down into small pieces you can achieve easily and start working toward that dream. Your dreams will change over time and that's okay. Just let yourself enjoy each small step as you achieve it. If you try to take too big of steps, you will fail and never achieve your dream. As you take each small step, you are one step closer to your dream and a new beginning. Don't get so intent on achieving your long-term dream that you fail to slow down and smell the roses along the way. We all have our life clock ticking, and the moment that just passed we will never get another chance to relive and replay. Therefore, do it right the first time and enjoy every minute of it.

For example, when I first started my own CPA firm, I thought the world would beat a path to my door because I had worked for a large CPA firm. That simply did not happen, so I began to look at all the steps I needed to put in place to make my firm profitable, such as determining the best way to get in front of people who did not know me. I determined that one way was to be a low bidder on any public bid work. Once I got the job, I super-served and gave the organization more advice and service than they expected. This little step resulted in the organization telling others what a great job I did, which led to more referrals and more competitive fees. The simple message is that it all ties back to lots of small steps, which all point to your dream, and each one gets you a little closer. In some cases you will fail, but you can learn from your failures just the same as your successes.

INTEGRITY: PIECES OF THE DREAM

To achieve your dream you must build integrity into your product, your processes, your customer relations, and everything about your business. Everything—from the quality of your products, to how you treat your employees, to how you treat your customers—has to be first class. When you see a stamp that says UL approved, you know that the Underwriters Laboratories has tested a product and you can trust that product. When people think of your business and your product, they need to have that same feeling of trust and integrity. To get that feeling, you have to understand some of the important steps to ensure quality and customer trust.

OFFER QUALITY

When people do business with you, they assume you will deliver the best product or service at the best price. You are the expert simply by being in business. However, you must realize the customer's perception of quality is often different from the business owner's. To understand quality, let's look at Six Sigma. It refers to the goal of having your quality standards so high that the error rate is approximately three in one million.

Honeywell International Inc. puts the engineers in their nuclear weapons division through this quality training to get the best results possible. If the United States ever has to use a nuclear weapon will you want it to destroy a target as designed or will you just want an above-average chance it will destroy the target? An error rate higher than three per million won't be acceptable in that scenario, and your customers view your product or service from the same perspective. They expect it to be the very best every time.

OFFER VALUE OVER PRICE

Good lumber ain't cheap, and cheap lumber ain't good. This is an excellent example of why we should always strive to provide superior products and/or services and not be afraid to price accordingly. If all you have to sell is price, then someone will always beat you at your game. When what you offer is the best, the world will be more willing to put a higher value on that. You also must constantly improve or the world will pass you by.

Help Others in Order to Help Yourself

It matters not whether you are dealing with a customer or an employee; you should always care about them and treat them the way you would want to be treated. If you want the best employees and the best customers telling others about you, then you must truly care about them. If you think about it, when you give others what they want, they will feel good about you and be glad to help you in return. In your mind don't always think of everyone from the perspective of "what can this person do for me?" Treat those who can do you absolutely no good the same way you treat those who you think can be a key to your success and you will go far.

The concept is very simple: If you truly care about others it will show in everything you do, and as you help others they will want to work for you and do business with you. Listen twice as much as you talk, and always answer from the viewpoint of the person to whom you are talking. Everyone likes to think they had a great idea. Your job is to drop enough hints so that they come up with the idea you had while feeling like it is theirs. That way everyone wins, because you get what you want and they feel good about how creative they were.

Follow the Rules

Think back to those times when you didn't want to report some income on your income tax return because you felt you were already paying more than your share to the government. Now put yourself in the shoes of the employees or customers when they see you pocket cash from the business or you tell them you don't have to report cash sales. What you have really done is told your employees or customers it is okay to not follow the rules. Now they think it is okay to do the same, but they may not take advantage of the tax man—they may take advantage of you. It is always better to follow the rules, and you won't ever have to defend an action you can't legally uphold.

BE THE BEST

To succeed at your dreams and build integrity, you must follow a common set of guidelines. Old habits are hard to break, but dreams and integrity are achieved with a consistent pattern of doing many small things right. By offering your customers quality and good value, helping others, following the rules, and being the best, your dreams of small-business success can come true.

Now that you have the basics, it is time to move on to selection of the business product or service you want to offer. It is always easier to go to work every day if you are doing something you feel good about.

Chapter 2

Pick the Right Business for You

By C. Gregory Orcutt, CPA

"Reasons people go into business: 41% joined family business, 36% wanted more control over future, 27% tired of working for others, and 5% downsized or laid off."

—Dun and Bradstreet
19th Annual Small Business
Survey May 2000.

How do you know what kind of business you should go into? There are so many different kinds, and the decision can be so overwhelming that most people never go into business for themselves. But if you have a passion for working for yourself, what you decide will affect you for your lifetime. You must spend a significant amount of time deciding on the business you will start. Also you will want to consult with some professional advisers. Many of you reading this book may be past this decision, but if not, read carefully. There is much to consider.

Use Your Experience as an Employee

Many people will start a business in an industry in which they are currently employed. Already having the expertise that is needed to provide the service or product is a great starting point. You will already have contacts and maybe some quick contracts or customers before the doors are even open. If you have a passion for the work you currently perform, creating a business around your passion can make this decision easy. We want to enjoy going to work each day, and it can be very satisfying to own a business where you love doing the work.

As an employee, you can often observe how you would *not* want to run a business. Perhaps it's how the product is made, the service performed, or a lack of customer service. You can see how to do it better. This can be a good starting point for your new business. You will quickly find out that being the owner is not as easy as it looks.

I have had many clients start their own businesses and significantly improve the results of their previous employer. One such client was able to build his new business to the point that his previous employer offered to purchase the new company. He did not sell but was proud of his accomplishments in taking what he had learned and improving upon it.

The alternative is to run a business different from where you started in your career. If you want to get a fresh start in a new industry, your learning curve will be steep. Starting over can be a great way to invigorate your career. You might have been working in a dead-end job and need a new challenge. Obviously you will have a lot to learn and a harder decision to make. Many people have done this successfully. Starting over can be exciting, but you will need to find people and resources that you can learn from and rely on for advice.

Determine Your Characteristics for Success

Whether or not you enter an industry with which you are familiar, you need to confirm that you are suited to owning a business. Just because you want to does not mean it is a good idea. We have seen many small businesses fail because the owner did not have the skills required for owning a business. Just having the technical skills to perform your trade or service is not enough. You need to consider all your strengths and weaknesses before starting.

The Small Business Administration (SBA) offers a list of characteristics that successful entrepreneurs possess:[i]

- Persistence
- Desire for immediate feedback
- Inquisitiveness
- Strong drive to achieve
- High energy level
- Goal-oriented behavior
- Independence
- Demanding attitude
- Self-confidence
- Calculated risk-taking tendency
- Creativity
- Innovation
- Vision
- Commitment
- Problem-solving skills
- Tolerance for ambiguity
- Strong integrity
- Reliability
- Personal initiative
- Ability to consolidate resources
- Strong management and organizational skills
- Competitive spirit

- Change agent
- Tolerance for failure
- Desire to work hard
- Luck

Good business owners do not possess all of the above traits, but you will need all of them at some time in your career. You will quickly learn which of these traits you do not possess so you can surround yourself with people who do. To build a successful business you will need a team. Your teammates will complement your weaknesses and you will complement theirs, so the team can have all the above attributes.

Make sure you pick a business you enjoy. You will be working long hours and sacrificing time away from family and friends. Be careful to choose a business that utilizes your natural talents. Don't start building houses if you can't work with your hands. If you have an analytical mind, take advantage of it.

STEPS TO SELECTING THE RIGHT BUSINESS

Once you have created a list of business possibilities, how should you narrow the list down to your final choice? What should you consider when making the final decision? In over twenty years of consulting with small businesses, we have found that successful business owners take the following steps when considering new business ventures.

1. Test your ideas. Start by running your ideas past other people. You should not look for people who will assume anything you do will be a success, like your mother. But run it by other professionals in a related business or people who may be potential customers. You want people to be honest and open, not just with your idea but how they view your abilities to succeed in your own business.

2. Identify your customer. Ultimately the success of your business will depend on how many customers you can attract. Therefore, you need to identify who those people are and what their patronage looks like. The more narrowly defined this group is, the better. By identifying your ideal demographic market, you can more easily start to project your financial results.

3. Give them what they want. You need to confirm that your customers are willing to buy what you are selling. Ask them to look at your idea and critique it. You will not be able to sell them a service or product that they do not want. Listen to their comments and be willing to adapt your ideas to what they need.

4. Count the cost. To be successful you will need to understand the amount of money you need to start your business and survive the first year. Create a budget that is flexible and considers the best- and worst-case scenarios. You do not want to be underfunded.

5. Determine who is on your team. What are the skills that are required to provide the service or product your business will offer? As the owner, you need to understand your limits and find other people who will complement you.

6. Consider the short term versus the long term. How long will your product or service be viable? Is technology changing rapidly? Are you working in a very competitive market? You need to consider the next product line or service that you will need to offer. Before going into business you need to understand how long you need to invest before you realize a return on your investment.

7. Plan an exit strategy. How long do you anticipate owning your business? When will you want to sell your business? Success does not always mean thirty years of owning a business. You might build the business and sell in five to ten years. Make sure your idea for your business matches the longevity of your business and your exit strategy.

As accountants we see many businesses come and go. We wish they could all succeed; however, many do not have a chance from the start. We have been surprised at some that make it and also surprised at some that do not.

Many of the businesses that struggle from the beginning are underfunded. You must prepare a budget for the first couple of years of your business. If you underestimate the funding you need, it's likely that you will not be able to obtain more. Banks will usually not lend to a new business that has not accumulated any equity. You might have heard of a successful business that started on a shoe string, but most that start that way don't make it. Plan to succeed by having the right amount of money available.

Choosing the right business for you is a crucial first step in succeeding with your new enterprise. Consider your current field, your past experience, and your current financial resources before making this important decision. The next chapter will help you evaluate yourself.

Chapter 3

Self-Evaluation for Small-Business Success

By R. Sean Manning, CPA

You've made it through the seven criteria and have selected a business that looks like a good opportunity. Congratulations! Now it's time to evaluate your skills, risk tolerance, and commitment.

Doing a self-evaluation is a critical step in deciding if you should start a business. To really be successful in starting a new business, you must take a close look at what it is going to take and determine if you have the time and resources to make your business successful.

Decision-Making Skills

Let's start by discussing quick thinking skills and critical thinking skills, two very different types of skills that may be needed to make the right decisions for you and your business.

First, do you have quick thinking skills? Those are skills that show your ability to think on your feet when faced with an immediate decision that might have a dramatic impact on your business. Generally people are faced with making tough decisions when they are put on the spot. As a leader of your business you will be tasked with constant circumstances that require your immediate response, and you will need to be able to make logical decisions under pressure. Often these immediate responses will play critical roles in your businesses success. Some things that might affect your decision-making process are how you were raised, your religion, political views, education, and your core beliefs.

The next type of decision you might be faced with making is that which requires critical thinking, more in-depth thought and deeper analysis. Critical thinking becomes much easier when you utilize training and other available resources to assemble relevant facts. This is one reason to keep building knowledge through reading books and articles, and also seek out knowledgeable people through relationships, organizations, professional contacts, and other business owners who can support you when you need to make a critical decision.

These are just two different situations. Keep in mind that thinking ahead and anticipating problems or questions will help put you in a better position to make the right decision. In general, try to avoid making a rush decision, but also show leadership and confidence in your decisions while admitting when you make a mistake. Keep in mind that sometimes you must also trust your gut instinct.

Risk Tolerance

Owning and operating your own business can have the appearance of either being a stable long-term opportunity or an extremely risky endeavor. Risk tolerance, which is the measure of uncertainty a person is willing to accept in respect to the perceived benefits, is why there is such a wide range of perceived risk in owning a business. The realization of owning your own business does have risks, and those risks can be mitigated by making good decisions and by being prepared.

Many studies indicate that entrepreneurs have a low tolerance for risk, which can appear contradictory to most people's perceptions. This appears to be so counterintuitive because most entrepreneurs also tend to be overconfident in their ability to be successful. This overconfidence gives the entrepreneur the ability to adapt and commit to tasks that most people would consider crazy, like working eighty hour weeks for weeks on end without any form of compensation. So, if you are risk averse, owning your own business might become very stressful and unmanageable unless you also possess a great deal of confidence in the success of your endeavor.

Your personality and risk can be assessed many different ways to provide a self-evaluation. The assessments generally consist of a series of questions and can be done by using a reputable online source or ordering a package that allows you to take and score the test. One of the most detailed is the DiSC® Assessment, which can be reviewed and purchased online from a number of sources, like www.TheDiSCPersonalityTest.com. Another good tool to consider is a career assessment test. These also can be researched and accessed online. One to consider is the Myers-Briggs® test, which is a career, personality, and leadership test. The last area of test you can consider is a hiring test for yourself. These will also provide good information on your personality and goals and help direct you to your areas of strengths and weaknesses in business.

Commitment and Passion

As accountants, we see many passionate people starting new businesses. Passion must be properly directed to a product or service that can produce a viable business. Many passionate people get caught up in the idea and not the truth of the idea's ability to sustain a business. If the idea has sustainability, the commitment behind it must be unyielding.

One's commitment can be tested in many ways when you own a business and often includes the drain on financial resources, the time to make a business successful, one's adaptability to unexpected changes, and even trust in the business itself. Proper budgeting will help prepare a business owner for the financial commitment, but it is the unanticipated sacrifices that come with owning your own business that give the true test of one's commitment. Seven-day workweeks for months are a true possibility for some new businesses. The challenge is to find ways to avoid having your business consume you, your family, and your money. Make good decisions on what can and should be delegated to professionals and employees. If you try to do everything, you might start to fail at the one product or service that is your business.

No doubt entrepreneurship is not for everyone. Our website, www.6stepstobusiness.com, has tools and resources that you can use for further information and deeper analysis. Be sure to do a self-evaluation so that you feel confident in your decision-making skills, assess what you are willing to risk to make your business successful, and are able to move forward with passion and commitment.

In addition to your self-evaluation you can get advice from a variety of skilled professionals, as you will see in the next chapter.

Chapter 4

Advisers for Your Business

By R. Sean Manning, CPA

Most often, even before a business opens its doors, the business owners have consulted and worked with professional advisers to draft agreements, such as buy/sell agreements, partnership agreements, and the like. Advisers will play many roles as you prepare to open the business's doors.

One common trait many successful business owners have is that they maintain a close business relationship with their trusted advisers. These advisers include accountants, attorneys, bankers, financial, information technology (IT), and other professionals. Advisers should be selected based on the business owner's skills and available resources. Obviously we all have different skills, and business owners must recognize the areas in which they might need professional advice and when it is appropriate to seek that advice. Far too often the decision not to hire and retain advisers is based on economics or the assumption that an adviser isn't affordable. In many circumstances the lack of proper advice can cost business owners thousands of dollars or even the loss of their business. For example, many business owners fail to consult with an attorney regarding employee relations or contractual documents for customers. That can lead to costly litigation when a question or problem arises that was not properly documented in the beginning. The stress and challenges around these problems can certainly become overwhelming to the business owner, causing distractions and challenges that can reduce the opportunity for the business to be successful.

Let's look at some advisers and the role they can play in supporting your business.

ACCOUNTANT OR CPA

Accountants can assist a business owner in a number of ways. They are usually familiar with the government agency requirements of setting up a new business. This might include filing for business and sales tax licensing along with initial recommendations relating to a multitude of questions a new business owner regularly has.

After the business is established, an accountant can assist with many of the accounting-related functions of the business. This includes properly prepared financial statements, bank reconciliation, sales tax preparation, payroll tax preparation, and other regulatory reporting requirements. Accountants can assist annually with the federal tax preparation and state reporting requirements. As the business matures, the business owner should discuss the business' needs with his accountant on a regular basis. Also, budgeting and even exit strategy planning will become key discussion items that the accountant will need to coach the business owner through. The accountant also is often a key player in the communication with the other advisers.

ATTORNEY

Attorneys are often looked to when a problem arises and legal advice is needed to help resolve the concern. They can also play an important role in the formation of the business and preparing documents that will help the business avoid future problems. If you as the business owner have elected to form a legal entity, such as a limited liability company (LLC), corporation, or partnership, there are many legal documents that might be required to properly establish and protect your business and its other owners. Many businesses require special regulation and unique legal considerations, so an initial consultation with an attorney for any new business is recommended. Additionally the attorney should be considered whenever the business is challenged legally. There are many specialties in law, and if a unique situation arises that requires specific legal assistance, the business owner would be wise to consult with the proper attorney to resolve the legal challenge.

Banker

During the life cycle of a business, there are usually numerous occasions that require additional capital. Financing may be required to start the business and support the business in the early years until a revenue stream can become large and consistent enough to maintain the business. As the business matures, a reliable banker can also support the business needs to acquire equipment, finance growth or develop new products. Well-managed financing can be the cornerstone of a successful business. Banks often go through lending changes, so regular correspondence with your banker is advised. The need for financing for the next five to ten years should always be evaluated to properly communicate the needs to your banker. This will help provide opportunistic planning that will lead to a simpler approval process and better conditions for financing. Also always discuss your bank's available services with your banker; many banks can provide you and your business with added services.

Financial Adviser

Financial advisers can play an important role during all phases of the business cycle. If a new business owner is funding the start-up of the business, his current financial portfolio will need to be managed to meet the short-term needs of the business. As the business matures, a focus on retirement and investment savings becomes a more important goal of the business owner. Therefore, the financial adviser should consider the various risks and needs of the business owner on a regular basis. Although it is important that all the business advisers stay connected, the financial adviser and the accountant should consider communicating with the business owner at least annually. Tax law changes and investment planning strategies often provide various planning opportunities throughout the business life cycle, which keep these two advisers connected. One final measure of a business's success can be the sale of the business, often providing substantial cash for the owner to invest.

Insurance Adviser

A wide range of insurance needs are common for a new business owner. Although more details are provided later in the book as to the different types of insurance, we want to remind the new business owner here to consider building strong relationships with the various insurance providers.

Information Technology (IT) Expert(s)

Not only do the traditional IT needs of a business, like hardware and software need to be considered and managed, but other important aspects—like information security, system backups, power supplies, internet providers, along with a host of similar technology-driven items—need to be evaluated. Most businesses collect a wide range of information for customers, employees, and other businesses. That information must be kept secure, and the risk of loss of such information must be mitigated. Consider partnering with an IT professional who not only can meet your immediate perceived needs but also provides direction in areas with which you might be unfamiliar.

OTHER ADVISERS

There are a number of other business-related advisers that can assist a business owner during the business' various phases and changing needs. They might include consultants, coaches, and marketing experts.

As with all your advisers, please evaluate not only your own needs and expectations but also the qualifications and experience of your advisers. Although most advisers have an interest in your success, some are also out there to take advantage of unsuspecting business owners. Ask for referrals, do your research, and find ways to measure your success in relation to your advisers. Your good decisions and strong, trusted adviser relationships generally spawn greater opportunity for success and help avoid costly mistakes.

Most qualified advisers have experience with franchises. The next chapter discusses the pros and cons of buying a franchised business.

Chapter 5

Buying a Franchise or Starting from the Ground Up

By R. Sean Manning, CPA

Most business owners start or join an independent business, others decide they stand a better chance for success by buying a franchise. If after reading this chapter you crave additional information consider more in-depth research on websites like www.franchising.com that help educate prospective business owners about the franchise industry including the Pros and Cons. Books like *Franchising in Canada: Pros and Cons* by Michael M. Coltman even provide additional statistical information about independent and franchise businesses.

Whether you have been consulting with trusted advisers or have just started your research, many prospective business owners will need to closely evaluate the decision to buy a franchise or take the more independent approach and start a business your own way.

Franchise: A business contract in which an independent business (the franchisee) sells or markets the products and/or services of a larger firm (the franchisor). The franchisee often receives training and marketing support from the franchisor and pays a fee for the ongoing support. Some franchises that you're probably familiar with are McDonald's®, Subway®, CITGO, Stanley Steemer, The UPS Store®, and Fantastic Sams®.

When prospective business owners work with a franchisor, they will typically go through more research and be exposed to greater planning that can lead to greater understanding of the business and a better opportunity for success. Also, the franchise can expose you to other business franchise owners who can share problems and solutions allowing you to be less prone to make the same mistakes they made. Owning a franchise can be like working with a good advisory team or mentorship team that can provide you a greater opportunity for your own business success.

A franchise provides prospective business owners with a systematic approach to business ownership that has been proven successful and is then basically packaged up for reproduction. The franchisor gives the franchisee a detailed list of procedures to follow that helps the franchisee start and manage the business. The franchisor also has strict guidelines that control the operations, products, and services of the franchisee. If the franchise is well managed, the franchisor can offer added value to the franchisee. The franchisor may be able to invest in marketing techniques that, for the franchisee, would be unattainable due to the pooling of resources. Some franchisors can also develop buying power and pass savings on to the franchisee.

Generally the start-up cost of a franchise is more than a similar type of non-franchise business due to the cost involved with paying the franchise fee and specific requirements the franchisor may have. Some non-franchise business owners may elect to postpone costs that most franchisors require prior to opening. The requirements of the franchisor are designed to take the risk out of starting a new business (which does not always happen—we can all recognize failed franchisees that have closed where we live and work). There is no sure thing when it comes to opening a business, even a franchise. Business owners themselves often play a key role in the success of the business.

Advantages of Buying a Franchise

Franchise businesses often eliminate some of the guesswork in starting and running a business. The franchisor will provide the framework for the new business, and other franchisees often become a primary source of information that is shared among the various franchisees.

Disadvantages of Buying a Franchise

The ongoing royalty fees that are paid to the franchisor are one area of franchise ownership that you should understand and be comfortable with. Some franchise owners perceive great value in the franchise fees and the ability to help their business. Others look at the franchise fees as an anchor. Be sure you understand what the royalty fees are and be sure you are comfortable with the payments, as they will generally be there for as long as you own the business.

Summary

Owning a business is a dream of many people, and a franchise provides that opportunity to thousands, if not millions, of business owners. To help determine if franchise ownership is right for you, do your research. Talk to franchisees and franchisors. Research what type of business you would like to own, and look at the risk involved.

Start your research by performing an online search of "most successful franchises" and "least successful franchises." The results change every year, so it will be important to do the research when you are considering franchise ownership. As you start to narrow your selection, dig deeper into your list of franchise considerations. Search online for ownership satisfaction statistics, customer satisfaction statistics, and industry statistics to help solidify your choice of franchise.

Your personality may help point you in the right direction. If you like a systematic, disciplined approach to owning and operating a business, a franchise might be a good option. If you resist conformity and thrive on creativity, you might be better off not committing to a franchise. Keep an open mind and evaluate all your options. Arm yourself with knowledge. When looking at business ownership opportunities, people tend to lean in one direction or the other, franchise or independent business. Both have advantages and disadvantages, and we hope this chapter helps lay the groundwork for helping you make the right decision.

The U.S. Census Bureau reported on Tuesday, September 14, 2010, that franchise businesses accounted for 10.5 percent of businesses, from data collected in 2007. Of the 4.3 million total establishments surveyed, 453,326 were either franchisee- or franchisor-owned businesses.[ii]

Now that you have decided what kind of business you want to own, it is time to start doing some more in-depth planning and business analysis. Whether you buy a franchise or start your own business from the ground up, your business will be more successful with a business plan.

Chapter 6

The Business Plan: Creating the Map to Your Success

By R. Sean Manning, CPA

Previously, in the chapter on franchises, we talked about the systems and fundamentals that are required by the franchisor to be a franchisee. These systematic approaches to starting a business are required because they help lead a new business to success. So why don't all business owners do thorough business planning? The answer is that they should. Whether they have chosen to buy a franchise or decided to create their own unique business, the next item on their to-do list should be extensive business planning.

Business Plan: A business plan is a formal document which describes the business, details the goals of the business, and describes how those goals will be attained as well as the risk factors that may present problems.

There are a number of resources available to help assist you in preparing a business plan. Too many business owners think they have a good idea and decide that a good idea warrants starting a new business. If business owners take the time to prepare a business plan, they might find that risk factors, originally undetected, become evident in the business plan and decide against starting a new business. It is far better to invest the time in writing a business plan than to invest more time and money in a failed idea. After the business plan is prepared and the business started, keep the business plan available and revisit it every couple years. Make updates to the plan and use it as a working document to help aid your success.

The Business Plan Overview

A business plan will typically be made up of the following elements. Use a step-by-step process similar to this when outlining key points:

1. Start with a description or story about the business. The description should go into some details and talk about your vision, the market, and the people involved with the business.
2. Include market analysis. This should be considered to fully understand the market opportunities and the competition that is currently present, along with potential future competition.
3. Prepare a SWOT report. A SWOT report is a short discussion on the Strengths, Weaknesses, Opportunities, and Threats of your business.
4. Include financial projections. Do this initially, to get the company started, and then prepare an annual budget for the first few years.
5. Include a marketing plan. This should discuss in more detail how you plan to market the business.
6. Detail key employees, daily operations, and staffing requirements. Again, discuss the business at start-up and for the first few years.

Books that may be helpful are:
Anatomy of a Business Plan: A Step-By-Step Guide to Starting Smart, Building the Business, and Securing Your Company's Future by Linda Pinson
Successful Business Plan: Secrets & Strategies by Rhonda Abrams
Writing a Convincing Business Plan by Arthur DeThomas Ph.D. and Stephanie Derammelaere, MBA.
See the Further Reading section for additional information.

BUSINESS PLAN INFORMATION

INDUSTRY PROFITABILITY AND INDUSTRY POTENTIAL

Later in the book we will discuss key operating statistics to understand how your business is doing against other businesses in the same industry. Before you start a business, it is also recommended that you study the industry to determine the profitability levels and the potential revenue in that particular industry. This type of research can be done on all types of industries and should provide valuable information.

Research on a particular industry can be challenging and takes time. Be creative, use not only online resources but also consider interviewing other business owners, search out industry associations, and speak to their members or look for organizations that publish industry data.

If you have developed a new or unique product or service, you might want to consider doing an analysis of a similar product or service in a different industry. By doing the industry analysis you will begin to understand what makes a particular business successful in its respective industry. That understanding might also give you a competitive edge that can lead to greater success.

MARKET SHARE AVAILABILITY

Market share availability is important because you need to determine what kind of demand for your product or service exists in the market. Some market share analysis can be local—for instance a restaurant or small retail store. Other types of market analysis might be considered at the regional, national, or even global levels. A market analysis can be summed up as a report that discusses the who, what, why, where, when, and how of the product or service that you will sell or deliver to the customer or consumer. The more detail you can provide in the report, the better you will understand your market and the opportunities for success.

ANALYSIS OF COMPETITION

Now that you studied the market share, you should have a good idea of who your competition is. You should study your competition to gain a competitive edge. When you have a competitive edge in business you create a greater opportunity for success. When you study the competition, think of yourself as a consumer, act like a consumer, and talk to your competitors' consumers. Try to learn about specific people in your industry and what their current strengths and weakness might be. This knowledge will not only help you gain a competitive edge now but will also prepare you to be competitive in a world that is changing more rapidly than ever.

CASH FLOW

A cash flow is different from a budget because a cash flow takes into account all sources of income. Most often business owners focus on the cash inflow from sales. In addition, cash can come from investors or lending sources. When you combine all sources of cash, you develop an understanding of the necessary funds needed to run and maintain a successful business. The reason you analyze sources of cash is that most businesses are faced with struggles or opportunities that will require cash. Being prepared and understanding what sources are available will help you position your business to be proactive rather than reactive when cash is needed.

Planning for your business can be a time-consuming task. Consider the benefits a well-thought-out plan will provide as you develop documents to not only support your business but also give you the opportunity to gather information and knowledge before you make the final decision to start your new business. This information might be what ultimately determines your success.

In addition to your business plan, a strategic marketing plan will help both you and any investors make decisions about where to focus your marketing efforts and spend marketing dollars. The next chapter reviews the components of this important document.

Chapter 7

Strategic Marketing Planning

By David J. Lucier, CPA

Strategic marketing planning is the most important component to achieving business success; however, it is also one of the most overlooked areas contributing to business failure. This chapter covers strategic marketing planning and tactical planning. A sample strategic marketing plan is included, which can be used as a quick guide to help you develop your own plan.

Businesses today operate in a complex, fast-paced, quick-changing environment. Marketing planning is a process for coping with these changes. Marketing is everything a company does to get in front of a customer whether it's face to face or via e-mail, website or the telephone. Most successful companies that I have seen are market driven and follow a long-term strategic plan.

The three-year strategic marketing plan is preceded by the annual tactical plan. The three-year strategic marketing plan is a written document outlining how the business is perceived in the market relative to its competitors, what the objectives are that will be achieved, what resources are required, and what results are expected. In my opinion, three years is the perfect window for planning. In today's fast-paced, quick-changing world, any plan longer than three years could make the plan only a guess.

The strategic marketing plan will be used by management to run the company and to stay focused on the goals. It will also help management communicate the strategy to investors and creditors. Not only must management write up the plan, but all key stakeholders must buy into the goals. This is usually done starting with a one- or two-day retreat followed by a number of follow-up meetings. The following are the major components included in the strategic marketing plan:

- **Mission Statement:** defines the company's core values, business definition, core competence, and future indicators.
- **Financial Summary:** summarizes the financial implications over the three-year planning period.
- **Market Overview:** provides a brief picture of the market including; structure, threats, and segments.
- **SWOT Analysis:** Strengths, Weaknesses, Opportunities, and Threats—the strengths and weaknesses of the business, the opportunities presented by its customers, products or services and the threats against it.
- **Assumptions:** must be tested as they relate to the marketing objectives and strategies.
- **Marketing Objectives:** defined by the profits, sales, value, and market share that the business wishes to achieve.
- **Marketing Strategies:** State how the objectives are to be achieved, which include product or service (the benefit to the customer), price (how it is priced to attract the right customers), place (who their customers are), and promotions (how they can be reached).

- **Budget Requirements:** broken down by year, by product, or service and are to include detailed revenue and costs associated.
- **Pricing:** High pricing can work against free referral marketing, and low pricing can erode profits. Value creation should drive your pricing model as well as competition.

TACTICAL MARKETING PLANNING

After your strategic marketing plan is completed, you'll want to have an annual tactical marketing plan, which is similar to a to-do list. This will cover what detailed programs will be implemented and include detailed scheduling and costing of tactics by year.

Successful marketing planning is the cornerstone of a solid, progressive, innovative, and profitable business. Given the rapidly changing business environment and high number of variables that influence profits, proper ongoing strategic marketing planning will enable a company's vision to become a reality. A detailed list of elements in a tactical marketing plan is included in Chapter 26. The timing of implementation, the budget for each element, and management responsibility should also be included.

SAMPLE STRATEGIC MARKETING PLAN

ABC123 Computers Inc.

1. MISSION

ABC123 Computers Inc. will focus on serving the small-business market located in Rhode Island and nearby Massachusetts. The company will provide hardware, software, and network support using a proactive service plan. This plan will preserve data integrity, minimize downtime, and maximize system usage and efficiency. The company will work with clients who want a strong service relationship and who value integrity of support.

2. Financial Summary (Projected)

	Year 1	Year 2	Year 3
Sales (Product)	$133,300	$200,000	$313,200
Hardware and Software Cost	$93,300	$140,000	$219,240
Gross Profit	$40,000	$60,000	$93,960
Service Revenue	$60,000	$90,000	$140,940
Gross Profit	$100,000	$150,000	$234,900
Officer Salary	$40,000	$60,000	$80,000
Payroll	$0	$0	$20,000
Payroll Taxes	$4,000	$6,000	$10,000
Professional Fees	$0	$3000	$7,000
Dues and Subscriptions	$500	$500	$500
Education	$1,000	$1,500	$2,000
Advertising and Marketing	$3,000	$6,000	$9,000
Office Expenses	$2,000	$2,000	$3,000
Insurance	$900	$1,200	$1,400
Telephone	$2,400	$3,000	$3,000
Auto Expenses	$12,000	$14,000	$18,000
Rent	$6,000	$7,000	$9,000
Miscellaneous	$2,000	$5,000	$7,000
Gross Expenses	$73,800	$109,200	$169,900
Net Income	$26,200	$40,800	$65,000

3. Market Overview

The current marketplace is represented by large, institutional companies who overcharge and have continuous technician turnover and weak relationship building. The smaller companies lack customer service and are limited in technical knowledge.

4. SWOT Analysis

Strengths
- Twenty-five years of experience
- Strong knowledge of hardware and networks

Weaknesses
- Needs more education on social network sites and search engine optimization

Recommendations: seminars, articles, and education

Opportunities
- Growing usage
- More consistency
- More processes
- More dependent on computers

Threats
- Disposable hardware
- Online software
- Remote support

Disposable hardware will reduce the need for an outside consultant. Online software will reduce the need for network consultants. Remote support will drive down the repair profits.

Recommendations: change with the times by serving what customers need.

5. Marketing Strategies

The following will be performed on an ongoing basis:

a. Develop a quarterly newsletter program that directly asks for referrals and additional work.
b. Build a strong relationship database.
c. Send handwritten thank-you cards to all referral sources.
d. Show up on time (ten minutes early).
e. Do what you say you are going to do.
f. Always say please and thank you.
g. Be proactive.
h. Develop a simple website.
i. Develop a thirty-second commercial, a way to ask for referrals, and a way to ask for more work.
j. Consider a letter-writing campaign.
k. Turn your business card into a mini brochure, and include it with all mailers.
l. Develop a referral postcard.
m. Consider joining a BNI® networking group.
n. Join local chambers, and make it a goal to give everyone your business card.
o. Consider telemarketing for appointment setting.
p. Consider hiring a part-time sales representative.

6. Pricing

Material pricing—gross profit will be 30 percent on items greater than $50 and 50 percent on items less than $50.

Labor pricing—will be $120 per hour with write-downs for rework and inefficient projects and write-ups for special knowledge learned from other clients or from continuing education. Develop proactive retainer pricing. Labor will make up 60 percent of the gross profit, and product sales will make up 40 percent.

In summary, a strategic marketing plan clearly outlines what steps you will take to market your business and promote sales. It is an invaluable document.

Marketing Books

The following marketing, relationship, sales, and strategy books have been hand selected after reading over two hundred books. These are the best ones for small businesses. Be careful when reading other books on the subject, because books written for medium and large businesses may lead you in the wrong direction.

1. *The Referral of a Lifetime: The Networking System That Produces Bottom-Line Results… Every Day! (The Ken Blanchard Series)* by Tim Templeton with Lynda Rutledge Stephenson
2. *Guerrilla Marketing: Easy and Inexpensive Strategies for Making Big Profits from Your Small Business*, 4th Ed. Jay Conrad Levinson with Jeannie Levinson and Amy Levinson
3. *Guerrilla Marketing for Free: Dozens of No-Cost Tactics to Promote Your Business and Energize Your Profits* by Jay Conrad Levinson
4. *Raving Fans: A Revolutionary Approach to Customer Service.* by Ken Blanchard and Sheldon Bowles
5. *Book Yourself Solid: The Fastest, Easiest, and Most Reliable System for Getting More Clients Than You Can Handle Even if You Hate Marketing and Selling* by Michael Port
6. *Purple Cow: Transform Your Business by Being Remarkable.* by Seth Godin
7. *Never Eat Alone: And Other Secrets to Success, One Relationship at a Time* by Keith Ferrazzi & Tahl Raz
8. *You Can't Teach a Kid to Ride a Bike at a Seminar: The Sandler Sales Institute's 7-Step System for Successful Selling* by David H. Sandler and John Hayes

9. *Close the Deal: 120 Checklists for Sales Success* by Sam Deep and Lyle Sussman
10. *Mr. Shmooze: The Art and Science of Selling Through Relationships* by Richard Abraham
11. *How to Win Friends & Influence People* by Dale Carnegie
12. *The Likeability Factor: How to Boost Your L-Factor and Achieve Your Life's Dreams* by Tim Sanders
13. *Endless Referrals*, 3rd Ed. by Bob Burg
14. *How to Become a Rainmaker: The Rules for Getting and Keeping Customers and Clients* by Jeffrey J. Fox
15. *Secrets of Great Rainmakers: The Keys to Success and Wealth* by Jeffrey J. Fox

Chapter 8

Partnerships and Agreements for Multiple Owners

By R. Sean Manning, CPA

The dedication of each owner to a shared vision is the first step in starting a successful partnership. Each owner might have a different personal goal, but the company goals and direction should be consistent to take the best advantage of opportunities. As a team, owners are combining forces to react more quickly and efficiently to business opportunities. The partners must be very cautious of others and avoid creating unnecessary tension that can begin to erode the advantages of the partnership.

Based on our experience, it is often this tension between partners that can create additional challenges that can eventually result in the failure of the partnership and can even result in the failure of the business. Long and prosperous partnerships are not always necessarily fair ones; the partners, however, have a strong understanding that as a group they are more successful than they can be individually. The partners often take on very different roles within the business, which creates diversity and the opportunity for each partner to be personally successful.

Because partnerships are faced with the risk of losing partners or disagreements among partners, it is highly recommended that the parties involved do some additional planning to try to avoid challenges that can not only tear apart strong personal relationships but also tear apart the business itself.

Communication

Although we can see the value of open communication between owners, there also needs to be a leader and decision maker for specific judgments or specific tasks. It might be related to divisions, such as operations or sales, or it might be assigned as an overall responsibility to a specific partner. Other decisions may require the collaboration of partners' opinions to come to an agreeable solution. It is often recommended that one partner or group of partners have a majority, at least 51 percent ownership, to avoid a deadlock on a decision. A deadlock can drain the energy from the partners and the business, causing obvious concern for the success of the business. If decisions cannot be made efficiently and with the trust of the partners, the business will have a difficult time maintaining a competitive edge.

Flexibility

Change is inevitable when it comes to business. All the planning in the world will not prepare you for the challenges that are created within a partnership. The understanding, commitment, and flexibility of the partners are what will determine the long-term success of the partnership. Sales could fall short or exceed expectations, staff might change, or key operational components might change. When these dramatic events occur, the flexibility of the partners and the business might be the most important aspect of the partnership to lead the business in a new direction for success.

Important Partnership Documents

Creating the proper documents is a required step for a partnership to be successful and deal with changes that occur during the life of the partnership. Nearly all partnerships will go through some kind of ownership change, and it is better to be prepared for the change rather than be reactive because your documents are not in order. Every year we consult with clients relating to changes to their partnership. These changes often involve family or close friends, and if the proper documents don't exist, these partnership changes can create so much tension that they ruin the fabric of the family relationship or friendship. Take the steps needed to create the following documents.

Partnership Agreement:
All partnerships should start with a partnership agreement. The partnership agreement can be made up of a number of separately described agreements. For example, the partnership agreement might include how the company will be funded and what each partner will be investing. It most often includes a general statement about the type of business the partnership will be conducting and may even provide details around the individual partners' job descriptions. Based on each partner's particular job, it will also talk about how partners are compensated and how profits and losses are split among owners. In addition to the general operations, the agreement should contain provisions as to how and when a partner's interest in the partnership is sold or purchased and when dissolution of the partnership would occur (Like a buy-sell agreement). A qualified attorney should be considered when drafting and reviewing the partnership documents. These documents help avoid litigation that can be very costly to the partners and the business.

The Center for Disease Control (CDC) provides studies and reports with detailed statistics on the success and failure rate of marriages in the United States. It would be interesting to see what type of information would be available if they were also able to study and report on the success of business partnerships.

It can be said a partnership is a bit like a marriage. You must trust, respect, and have the commitment to work together for a common goal. It is also common to hear that a partnership will never last, which is true because we will either outlive the business or the business will outlive us. Here are some pointers on making a business partnership last:

Ten Ways to Make a Partnership Last
1. Never insist on being right.
2. Work with your partner; teamwork is the key.
3. Start with rules and review documents when necessary.
4. Don't embarrass or criticize your partner in front of others.
5. Be communicative, not confrontational.
6. Recognize mistakes, but forgive and move on to new business.
7. Embrace challenges and work together to resolve them.
8. Share in the successes of the partnership.
9. Don't let outside distractions affect the goals of the partnership.
10. Be positive, have fun, and applaud your partner's efforts.

Especially for partnership-based businesses, advisers are typically very helpful in uncovering areas that need to be researched, discussed and, if necessary, documented with agreements among the partners. Although partnerships are unique and very popular, there are also other business forms and structures that are discussed in the next chapter.

Chapter 9

Business Format and Tax Structure

By C. Gregory Orcutt, CPA

Every business owner needs to make a decision about the business format and the tax structure within which they will operate. Make this decision before your business begins. The options include sole proprietorship, partnership, limited liability company (LLC), or corporation. Each of these is taxed differently. You will need to consult with your attorney and accountant to confirm that your business format provides you with the best liability protection appropriate for your business. Changing this format is possible in later years, but you will spend more money in professional fees and possibly taxes than making the best long-term decision at the beginning.

The business format choice is made first for legal reasons and second for tax reasons. Forming a separate entity to operate your business helps to keep legal problems restricted to the assets of your business and prevents them from affecting the owner's personal assets. In today's business environment, the two most popular choices are an LLC or a corporation. Due to the flexibility of organizing an LLC and less stringent annual record-keeping requirements, many new businesses are formed as LLCs. Other entity choices are a general or limited partnership or a sole proprietorship. Neither of those options will provide the legal liability protection that the corporation or LLC provide.

The simplest business format for a business owner is the sole proprietorship. Similar to the partnership, it does not offer any legal liability protection. Many businesses that start as a hobby or second job may use the sole proprietor entity but should always be considering the change to either an LLC or a corporation. The ability to separate the owner's personal net worth from the business' is a major advantage in forming an LLC or corporation. Once a business is using either employees or independent contractors, the owner should consider the change to a separate legal entity for the business. The potential of someone misrepresenting the business fraudulently, or ethically, significantly increases as the business grows. Insurance coverage is very important and will be covered in Chapter 18, but keeping the business as a separate entity is the first line of defense.

We recommend that a business selects a business format before the business starts. Unfortunately we have worked with many businesses that never form the separate entity and get too busy to make the decision later. Spending the time and investing the money in the beginning will be easier than doing it after the business is running.

BUSINESS FORMS AND TAXES

Making the business format choice should be done with both your attorney and accountant so that both the legal liability and tax consequences are considered. Everyone starting a business anticipates having profits quickly. Of course, you will have to pay taxes on those profits, but good planning will help minimize how much you pay. Each of these business formats are taxed differently.

There is not one answer for every business, so working with your team of advisers will help you sort through the options.

There are two major tax characteristics of any business format. Either the tax on the profits will be paid by the business or the profit will flow through to the owners who pay the tax personally. The major advantage of a flow through tax entity is that the profit will be taxed once on the owners' individual tax return. Businesses that pay the tax themselves may create another tax that the owners will pay from their salaries.

One advantage an LLC has over a corporation is that it can choose the method of taxation. There is not an LLC tax return form. A single-member LLC can choose to be taxed as a sole proprietor, a C corporation, or an S corporation. A multimember LLC could choose from a partnership, a C corporation, or an S corporation. It is important to keep the business format separate from the tax form that is filed. The flexibility of the LLC can create some confusion, but overall it is a good business format choice.

Tax Returns and Filing

Here are details about tax forms and how each of the business forms are taxed.

Sole proprietors will file a Schedule C on their personal income tax return, which is a simple income statement for their business. In addition to paying the 15.3 percent self employment tax that is comprised of Social Security and Medicare, the taxable profits will also be subject to federal, state and any related local income taxes for the owner. The owner will be taxed on the profits of the business, not based upon how much money the owner draws from the business. Often the amount the owner draws and the taxable profits are not the same number, so an accurate accounting throughout the year is important to prepare for the tax that will be due.

Partnerships file a Form 1065 federal income tax return. Most states and some city or county jurisdictions also have partnership tax returns. The taxation of the partnership is very similar to the S corporation. The differences are that a partner does not take a salary but withdraws the profits as they are available. All profits allocated to a non-passive owner may be subject to the self-employment tax. There is not an easy way to separate the income that is subject to employment taxes verses the business profits, like there is in an S corporation. One advantage partnerships have over corporations is that they are able to allocate the profit or losses to the owners with a different percentage than the ownership percentage. Generally a business with passive investments, such as real estate investments, would choose to be taxed as a partnership. Non-passive businesses that have owners working in the business would normally elect to be taxed as an S corporation.

S corporations file a Form 1120-S federal income tax return. Most states and some city or county jurisdictions also have corporate tax returns. This return reports the profits of the business and how much profit each owner needs to report on their individual income tax returns. The profit is reported on the owners' Schedule E and is not subject to the self-employment tax. The owners will include this income with all other taxable income and pay tax based upon their individual tax rate. If there is a loss it will flow through to the owner's individual income tax returns and, depending on the owner's basis, may be allowed to offset other income.

A simple definition of "basis" is the total of the money originally invested plus the taxable profits and less the tax losses each year and less the profits distributed to the owners. The basis calculation is one of the more complex issues in S corporation taxation. A schedule of the owners' basis needs to be maintained from year to year.

The owners that work in the S corporation business (not just investors) are required to take a reasonable salary. These wages are subject to all the taxes any other employee is required to pay. One of the biggest issues for an S corporation is how much the owner's salary should be compared to the profit distributions. Because the profit distributions are not subject to employment taxes, there is an advantage in paying out the profits rather than paying a salary. However, the tax law requires that a reasonable salary be paid to all working owners. You will want to discuss with your accountant the appropriate allocation of salary and profit distributions for your business.

To elect to become an S corporation, you must file a Form 2553 within seventy-five days of the start of the tax year. If the election needs to be made after that deadline, there are many exceptions where the IRS may allow a late filing. There are some rules that would not allow a C corporation or LLC owner to elect to be an S corporation. For example, all owners must be either U.S. citizens or U.S. residents. There are other requirements to qualify as a small business corporation that must be met before you can make the S corporation election. But with some planning with your advisers, most small businesses would easily qualify.

C corporations pay tax on the businesses profits by filing a Form 1120 federal income tax return. Most states and some city or county jurisdictions also have corporate tax returns. The C corporation will pay the tax on the profits based upon the federal corporate income tax rates that start at 15 percent for the first $50,000 of profit and go as high as 35 percent for profits over $100,000. If the owners of a C corporation decide to distribute profits to the owners as a dividend, an additional tax will be paid on the owners' personal income tax return. Because the same profits can be taxed twice, most small businesses will not want to be taxed as C corporations but rather as S corporations or partnerships. Most small-business C corporations will pay bonuses to the owners before year-end to eliminate or greatly reduce the profits. You must have an up-to-date accounting system in place to be able to make this decision before the end of the year. If the business has a loss, no tax will be paid and it will be used to offset either past or future years' profits. Estimated tax payments must be made by the corporation each quarter to all the taxing agencies.

If your business is in a separate business form, make sure that personal expenses are not comingled with business expenses. If an LLC or corporation is not run separate from the owners' personal and household expenses, you will lose the liability protection. If your home mortgage, utilities, or credit card bills are paid from the business checking account, you run the risk of "piercing the corporate veil." If you hear that term in court, it means the judge does not consider that you have formed a separate entity, so your personal assets may be at risk. This is very easy to avoid by making sure all personal expenses are paid from your personal checking account and business expenses from the business checking account.

Owners of flow-through entities must pay their taxes each quarter with estimated tax payments. An S corporation owner will also have income tax withheld from their paycheck. It is very important that the estimates are paid to meet the safe-harbor rules so that penalties are not paid. You must meet one of two rules to avoid paying a penalty for underpaying your income taxes. Either you pay in 100 percent (or 110 percent if your adjusted gross income is over $150,000 on a joint tax return) of your prior year's tax paid evenly throughout the next year or pay at least 90 percent of the tax that you will owe for the year. For example, if in the last tax year your total tax was $8,000, then you will make four quarterly payments of $2,000 on the fifteenth of April, June, September, and January. Or if you estimate that your taxes will be $10,000 for the year, you need to pay at least $9,000 throughout the year and pay the balance when you file your tax return. Keep in mind that if you pay what you paid last year but the current year is more profitable, then on April 15 when you file your tax return, you will owe more tax. Not only that, but you will also owe the first quarterly payment for the new year, which will be higher than the last year's payments.

FIGURE 9.1 BUSINESS FORMATS AND TAXES

	Sole Proprietorship	Partnership	S Corporation	C Corporation
Net Income	Included on owner's form 1040	Included on partners' form 1040	Included on shareholders' form 1040	Tax paid by corporation
Tax form	Schedule C on 1040	1065	1120-S	1120
Capital Gains	Owner pays at capital gain rates	Passes to partners and pays at capital gain rates	Passes to shareholders and pays at capital gain rates	Corporation pays at ordinary tax rates
Capital Losses	Owner offsets other capital gains plus deducts $3,000	Passes to partners; treated the same as sole proprietor	Passes to shareholders; treated same as sole proprietor	Only deductible against other corporate capital gains
Owner's Wages	N/A	N/A	Treated as other employees	Treated as other employees
Profit Distributions	All income taxed as ordinary and is subject to self-employment tax whether distributed or not	All income taxed as ordinary and may be subject to self-employment tax whether distributed or not	Profits taxed as ordinary income whether distributed or not	Taxed as dividends on the shareholders' 1040

Business forms and their tax consequences warrant special attention and advice from professionals. This is not the time to do it yourself!

Do not let taxes put you out of business. Too many businesses fail because they do not consider how much tax they will owe. Tax planning should be done throughout the year so that there are no surprises when you file your income tax return.

Chapter 10

Business, Family, and Personal Relationships: Making Them Work

By Bert Doerhoff, CPA

In this first section of the book, we talked about things you need to consider prior to going into business. In addition to the business, however, you'll want to consider your family and personal life, and keeping them working too.

When you have a business you enjoy, it is so easy for the business to consume your life. So before you address the systems you need to run your business, you first need to coordinate life and business. This chapter is about how to make sure you run your business and don't let the business run your life. In the scheme of everything it takes to succeed in business, the advice in this chapter may be some of the most difficult to enact.

As you climb the ladder of success, you will find the climb speeds up if you work on your job and not in it and if you work smarter and not harder. By working on your job you need to rethink how you do things to make sure you are always taking the most efficient and best route. Whereas when you simply work in your job, you tend to be like a robot, going through the same motions you went through in the past. Those who work in their jobs will often use the argument, "That is the way we've always done it."

Don't be afraid to rethink the old rules to improve on anything. There are two key concepts to consider here. First is how to make smart decisions about running the business. Second is coordinating personal and business life.

Make Smart Decisions in Running the Business

Most people go into business because they are technically very good at what they do. However, it is important to know what you don't know. Henry Domke, a very successful photographer in a very specialized field of photography, put it best. Henry said, "People think I spend all my time in photography. Actually, I only spend 25 percent of my time on anything to do with photography. The other 75 percent is running the business, marketing, communications, and all the daily administrative work of business." Thinking through what Henry said, I realized he put in very simple terms the reason most businesses fail. Most entrepreneurs are good at what they do, but they have no clue what else it takes to run a successful business. Thus, they only master 25 percent of what it takes to have a successful business. Anyone with their own business needs to step back and make sure they work *on* their business and not *in* their business.

Spend Time with Your Unique Ability®

Strategic Coach® is an entrepreneurial coaching organization that works with successful individuals to help them increase their income while also increasing their free time. One of the concepts taught by Strategic Coach is "Unique Ability," which is the essence of what you love to do and do best, in all areas of your life. It is a tool that identifies your unique talent and passion, and allows you to create value with maximum satisfaction and success. It's important for you to focus solely on your Unique Ability® Activities™ and to delegate any tasks that do not fall into your area of Unique Ability to others who do have a Unique Ability in those areas. This frees you up to focus only on what you do best, leading to higher productivity, greater results, and a more enjoyable way of life.[iii] For more information on the Strategic Coach® program and the Unique Ability® concept, please visit their website www.strategiccoach.com.

Take Your Family and Friends with You

Family and friends are number one. As the author who had to put this section to words, I had to look back at my personal life. The person from whom I learned the most about life is my wife and best friend. I must admit I was a slow learner and I probably failed more courses than she cares to admit, but she taught me that family is truly the most important part of life. I always wanted my kids to be perfect because, of course, I was, and rather than let them experience things for themselves, I always wanted to do things for them or correct things when they got done. Over time I finally learned that the best way to learn is through our own failures. I also realized that if we didn't have time for our kids when they were young, why should we expect them to want to make time for us later in life? If you only take one piece of advice from this book, take this one I learned from my wife: There is nothing more precious in life than family, and no one ever said on their deathbed that they wished they had worked more.

Understand It Is Not about You

On a recent business trip we were with a very successful business owner, and during our conversations he spoke of the time he held a gun to his head but at the last second could not pull the trigger. He had been an extremely successful salesman, and the company he worked for assigned him a private jet in which he would fly around the country to give motivational talks. One day his wife told him he either needed to give it up or he would have no family, so he decided to retire to farming his one thousand-acre farm. Six months later, when there were no longer any crowds and no one looked up to him at every turn, he decided to commit suicide because there was no longer any value to life. As he sat with the gun to his head, he heard the Lord tell him, "If you stop taking all the credit and start giving the credit, I will give you all the riches you could ever want."

After that he started his own very successful business, which today he has handed over to his children, and he now spends a lot of his time doing charitable work and helping others. We all like to feel indispensable, but in reality we are not the most important people in other people's lives. It is not about you!

In summary, you need to understand that a successful business involves so much more than being a very good technician. You need to learn the other 75 percent of what it takes to run the business and regularly set uninterrupted time to work *on* your business and not *in* your business. Then, once you go home, make family the same priority you made your business when you were at work, and understand the world does not revolve around you. As a business owner, if you implement the items discussed in this chapter you will experience what others have found. You will have a substantial increase in profitability of your business and a substantial increase in time off for personal life.

Now that you have a basic understanding of the lifestyle adjustments that come with successful business, let's get to the daily details of running the business. No business operates without a good understanding of financing, so let's start there.

Step 2:

Start-Up: Finances, Budgets, and Numbers

Chapter 11

Business Loans: A General Overview

By Lowell Lillge, CPA

For any business, cash is necessary. For a business that is just starting, or a business that has been around a while but is looking to expand, or one that is approaching a season where it must add more inventory or employees, money in the bank is crucial. If the business has the cash on hand, that is terrific. However, there will be times when there is not enough cash immediately available to cover these periods.

When those times arise and the money can't come from the owner's pocket, then cash from outside the organization must be found. That's where a loan can come into play.

Loan Types

Loans can come from a variety of sources: a bank, a family member, a friend, or another individual, to name just a few. These sources will give you the needed cash if you promise to pay it back within a certain time, along with something extra (interest) for the lender's benefit. Please remember that a loan from family or friends has to be handled the same way as a loan from a bank. Make sure all parties are in agreement as to how it will be paid, over what time, and what interest will be paid. Then stick to the agreement. You don't want this agreement to cause friction between the parties. Your ongoing relationship with family and friends is more important than getting a loan from them.

The time in which a loan can be repaid can vary. It may be short-term (within ninety days) or long-term (thirty years). The short-term loans will be repaid with funds that come into the business within that period. Most of these types of loans are best for inventory buildup for the busy season or some other investment that will have a quick payback. Longer-term loans are used for purposes for which the payback will take more than a year. One example of this is a building that will be used by a tool-and-die shop for its manufacturing facilities.

There are both secured and unsecured loans. **A secured loan is one that has collateral backing it up.** That means that if you can't pay back the loan, the lender can take your collateral. Period. You don't pay, and you don't get to keep your collateral. If you put up an automobile as collateral, you lose it. If you put up your house as collateral, you lose it. As you can see, it's pretty important to pay back the loan. **An unsecured loan has no collateral to back it up.** So, if you don't pay, you don't lose anything.

You may find that only the most credit-worthy and trusted businesses could even think about getting an unsecured loan. The lender will have to have a long and blemish-free record with the debtor before even considering this. Small businesses, unfortunately, are usually not in this group. For example, when banks extend a loan to a business, they usually require collateral (most often the item purchased with the proceeds of the loan) as well as the personal guarantee of the business owner. That means that if the business cannot make the loan payments, you must personally pay the loan as the personal guarantee.

Lender Concerns

Lenders don't really want your collateral. They deal with money. They want you to repay the loan under the terms of the agreement. Part of your repayment is interest, which is how they make their profit. It is easier for them to make that profit if they just deal with money. It is not easy for them if they have to seize your equipment and sell it. They aren't in the business of selling equipment. How do they know exactly what it should be sold for? If they seize it for future sale, now they have to learn something new—how to sell it and for how much. This takes time and costs them money. Extra costs cut into their profits. It just doesn't help their bottom line when they have to take this route. However, as you well know, they *will*, if there is no other way to get the loan principal back.

Lenders consider a number of factors when deciding whether to make a loan. A few of them are collateral, credit history, cash flow of the business, and management. We've already discussed collateral. Credit history means just that: What has the business done with prior loans? Were there any repayment problems? When looking at cash flow, they want to be sure that the loan will be repaid, on time, with interest. How profitable is the business? Is the business currently generating enough cash to make the payments? Will the use of the loan proceeds generate enough future cash to make the payments? Management is another important factor. Are the people running the business very good at what they do, or are they a bunch of dopes who don't have a clue but have only made it this far due to divine intervention?

Earlier, we mentioned interest. Interest is the charge you pay the lender so that it will give you the loan. This is its income, its sales. Interest charges for a business loan are going to be higher than for your home mortgage. Your mortgage is collateralized by your home. That building will be there for many years; therefore, the risk the bank is taking on the loan is not as great as it will be for a business loan. A business' value can fall dramatically, or the business might even go out of existence (as a result of some of the decisions made by the dopes referred to above). Because the lender has to take on more risk with a business loan, it will charge more than it would for a mortgage loan.

Lender A might quote you a certain interest rate, while Lender B will quote you a higher one. Lender A gets your business, right? Well, not so fast. There are other things to consider, like fees. Some lenders will quote a low interest rate, but after you figure in the fees, your monthly payment could be higher than another one. You should always look at what your total monthly payout will be. If there are fees to be paid up front, it might be good for you to look at the total amount you will pay the lender over the entire term of the loan. If you're going to look at dollars and cents, you might as well look at the total.

Another question to ask is; are there going to be any early payment penalties? See what the lender says. If your business is more profitable than expected, it would be good to pay off the loan early. This will save you money in the long term. Why should the lender penalize you for being profitable and paying the loan early? If the lender says it's because it will not be receiving interest on the loan, I consider that baloney, because the lender can just turn around and use that cash for a new loan to someone else. Now don't get me wrong. It probably won't happen, but just be aware of some of the things you have to consider.

Here is another thought on early payment penalties. Some banks may charge them. Others may not. These penalties, if they are to be enforced, are usually on commercial (business) loans. It would be to your advantage not to have early payment penalties as a condition of your loan. Why? Because, if you are able to pay the loan off early, you will be saving interest payments that will not have to be paid to the bank. That interest can be kept in the checkbook and used for something else that will benefit the business.

Probably the most important part of a loan is your relationship with your lender. You have to know him, and he has to know you. It takes time to get comfortable with each other, to build a trusting relationship. Start working on that now. The earlier it starts, the friendlier the lender will feel toward you when it comes time to approach him for the loan. It's always good to have him on your side before a need develops.

LINES OF CREDIT

Sometimes businesses have a need for cash beyond what is in the checking or savings accounts. Examples of this are: when accounts receivable are not being collected as timely as needed, when overdraft protection is needed on the checking account, when vendors are running discounts on inventory items needed by the business, and when unexpected repairs on machinery come up. Cash may also be needed to provide liquidity during the ups and downs of the business' normal operating cycle.

What is the business to do in a situation like this?

If the expense is small enough or the payback period is short enough (as in the case of inventory), a credit card or a line of credit (LOC) could be a good choice. Longer-term loans probably would not be a good choice since the business could be making payments for a longer time than necessary. Another thing about long term loans is that, even if all the funds are not needed immediately, the full amount *will* be disbursed to the business right away, and interest will be charged on that full amount.

So, just what is a line of credit?

An LOC is an agreement with a credit facility (usually a bank) that allows a business or person to take funds from the bank and repay them when the borrower wants to or has the ability to make the payments. A limit is preset as to how much can be borrowed, and a time is set as to when the total loan amount should be repaid, but otherwise the draws and loan principal repayments are pretty flexible. Having said that, be aware that interest payments have to be made each month on the outstanding loan balance. You might be familiar with a home equity LOC (HELOC). This is a personal LOC that utilizes the equity in your home as collateral for the loan.

Interest rates can be fixed or floating (also called adjustable), and they are usually based upon an index (such as the prime interest rate plus a percentage), which could vary by bank. The LOC's interest rate will also be lower than a credit card.

Here's an outline of the general steps that need to be taken in order to get an LOC:

Determine how much you are going to need. Be sure your calculations are accurate and that you are not erring on the short side. It's better to set up an LOC for an amount higher than will be needed rather than have to go back to your banker with your tail between your legs asking for more money. They'll be easier to work with by asking for more right away than having to explain why you made a mistake in your original request.

Talk to your banker about establishing an LOC. Your banker will be able to tell you what type of information the bank requires to extend credit to the business. One of the items the bank will require is your business plan. This will inform the bank of your ability to repay the principal and interest from the additional cash flow financed by the LOC.

Give the bank all the information it needs. It may seem to be a lot, but by cooperating with your banker you are making his job easier, which may make the overall approval process quicker and easier on you.

One last point about a line of credit: The best time to set up an LOC is *before* you need it. So do it now.

SMALL-BUSINESS ADMINISTRATION LOANS

What is a business owner to do when money is needed in the business, yet it's not in the checkbook, the bank won't lend anything (further), or the owner's personal situation can't provide any additional funds? An owner may want to consider an SBA loan as an alternative.

The U.S. Small Business Administration (SBA) was created in 1953 to help small businesses grow and prosper. SBA has a number of programs that are available to small businesses, but probably the most recognized is the financial assistance available through the SBA loan.

SBA loans can be used by businesses to purchase commercial real estate, renovate existing buildings, purchase equipment and inventory, acquire, expand, or start up a business, refinance an existing debt, or supply working capital.

SBA does not usually make loans directly to businesses or individuals. Rather, SBA guarantees a portion of the loan that a lender makes to the borrower. That portion ranges between 50 and 85 percent. This guarantee helps make the lender more comfortable with extending the loan in the first place. And if there is more comfort on the lender's part, there is more chance that a loan that the lender would not have made (due to poor collateral or the fact that it may be a start-up business) *will* be made.

SBA doesn't issue blanket guarantees on loans, so a business plan may be requested to accompany the loan request. A good conversation with your accountant will help you get the business plan ready for analysis by the bank and SBA.

Since the loans are made by the lender, repayment is also made to the lender.

Why should someone consider a loan guaranteed by SBA? Sometimes finance companies, savings and loan associations, and banks are reluctant to extend credit to small businesses no matter how pressing the need or how secure the financial position of the business appears. Lenders might be concerned about the ability of the borrower to repay the loan, or the value and type of collateral the borrower has, or they may even be concerned about the possibility of criticism from the bank examiners. There are a number of reasons to consider an SBA loan such as; longer repayment periods, no prepayment penalties, lower down payments, no balloon payments, and no points paid to the lender.

When SBA guarantees the loan, the lender is more likely to extend the loan, sometimes under more favorable terms than if it had made the loan by itself. What would make the terms more favorable? A longer repayment term, for example, or possibly a lower interest rate would make the loan easier for the business to pay back.

The interest rate is tied to the prime interest rate which is set by the Federal Reserve and reported by the Wall Street Journal. It could range from prime plus 2.75 percent to prime plus 4.25 percent. SBA charges points up front on the general loan as well as a monthly servicing fee, which is usually around 0.5 percent of the portion of the loan that it guarantees. This fee is charged to the lender, and the lender typically builds this into the rate.

Not everyone qualifies for an SBA loan. SBA considers collateral, the owner's contribution, and management capability before agreeing to underwrite a loan. The owner must also be of good character and never convicted of a felony. SBA also expects the loan to be repaid out of the profits of the business. Since SBA is mainly considered to be a cash flow lender, they look closely at the ability of the business owner to repay the loan. Furthermore, the owners may be required to give a personal guarantee (if they own 20 percent or more of the business).

While the acceptance process by SBA may be quick (just a few working days), the whole process from application to disbursement of the loan funds will take longer. That's because before SBA gets the application, the business must gather all the necessary data for the application, prepare the business plan, discuss it with the lender, and then send it in. So, businesses should prepare for loans well in advance of actually needing the funds.

BUYING VERSUS LEASING: ANOTHER FINANCING OPTION

With apologies to William Shakespeare, it's a question that keeps coming up: To buy, or not to buy? Whether you're discussing commercial real estate, a fleet of company cars, or business equipment, the answer is; it depends.

Many factors enter into answering this question. Even though the general factors are the same, they will apply to each individual and business in a different way. For some, a factor will be an advantage, and for others the same factor will be a disadvantage.

Let's take a look at the differences between leasing and buying.

One thing to consider is whether the asset will be kept for a relatively short time or a long time. A good example of this is a computer system. Some businesses might need to stay on the bleeding edge of technology. In other words, everything in their computer system has to be as up-to-date as possible. There can be no lag between what they are using and what's available in the marketplace. Since computer technology can change at such a rapid pace, leasing would be a good decision for this company. However, if the applications (programs) that a business is using will suit it for years to come, and if the computer itself (hardware) performs at a speed acceptable for years to come, purchasing might be the appropriate way for this business.

The building that will house the business also comes into play. If the business is in a growth mode, a lease might be the best option. That way it will be able to move to larger quarters when necessary. However, if the business is relatively stable with no need for additional space in the future, purchase of the building might be the best option.

Personal preference is another item to consider. You might prefer to have a new car every two or three years. All you have to do when the lease period is over is drop the old car off at the dealership and pick up the new one. Well, there is also the paperwork for the new car, but …

When a car is leased, the lease is determined on a set number of miles that you will be allowed to drive without incurring additional mileage charges. If you go over that mileage allowance, there will be an additional charge for each mile. If the number of miles you drive over the estimate is not very many, the charge should not be too much. However, if you really blow the estimate, there could be a substantial extra charge. So if you're thinking of leasing a vehicle, be pretty sure of how far you will be driving it. If you know you're going to drive a lot, or if you don't need a new vehicle every few years, you might find that a purchase is your best option.

Another consideration is payment. With a purchase, payments will cease at some point in time. With a lease, there will always be a payment due next month.

If you're looking at leasing or buying real estate (land and/or a building), appreciation might be a factor. With a purchase, there is the possibility that the value of the real estate may increase during the time you own it. When you sell it, you may realize a profit. With a lease of that same real estate, you have no possibility of realizing any appreciation. All appreciation stays with the owner, not the lessee. You should also be aware that there is the possibility of the value of the real estate decreasing at the point in time when you are ready to sell.

A purchase of an item will usually require a greater down payment than a lease. In the case of real estate, a purchase may require between 10 and 25 percent of the initial purchase price. This will vary depending on your lender. A lease of real estate, such as an office, usually requires a cash outlay of the first and last months' rent. As you can see, immediate cash available can be a big factor.

To buy or not to buy—that is still the question. But at least now you have some factors to consider.

Chapter 12

Another Use for Your Business Plan

By Lowell Lillge, CPA

"If you don't know where you're going, any road will get you there."
—Lewis Carroll

What in the world does this mean? I think it means you can either control where you're going or where you're going can control you.

Which would you prefer? If you own a business, I think you already know the answer. If you didn't want to be in charge of your own destiny (where you're going), why would you have put yourself in that position?

Do you have a business plan? If you do, you have control over where you're going. You have your road map. If you don't, you have no control over where you're going.

We won't get into a discussion of how to prepare your business plan here (that information is provided in Chapter 6), but I will give you one other use for it: to help you secure a business loan.

When you go to your lender to get a business loan, you have to convince him that the loan to your business does not carry a lot of risk with it. You have to convince him the loan is a good investment for him. He has to agree that giving you the money is a win-win situation. One of the items that will help convince him is your business plan.

There are a number of important pieces of information in the plan that will affect whether he feels he will be able to extend the loan to you. The following are just a few:

1. How much money do you need? Be sure of this amount. Make sure you are covering all the expenses you will run into. If you're just starting up the business your business plan should estimate good results and bad results, as well as what you really figure will happen. Discuss these possibilities with the lender so that he is aware of them.
2. Why do you want the loan? What are you going to do with it? Will it be spent on start-up expenses, on a building, on equipment (what type), or on something else? This information will help him tailor the best loan for your business.
3. How are you going to repay the loan? You will be able to show how the loan will be repaid and when with your projected cash flow statement. The lender will see that the loan proceeds will be put to good use, that the loan will help the overall profitability of the business, and that it will provide more than enough cash to pay him back.

If your plan is not able to answer these three questions, I'll guarantee that your business will not get the loan.

Your business plan isn't just used to get a loan. It's much more valuable than that. Use it to direct your business where you want it to go. Use it to compare what you wanted to happen to what is actually happening. Use it to make necessary midstream corrections. Use it to answer the questions your lender will have.

In the next chapter, we'll discuss those crucial financial statements; how to read them, and how to extract crucial information from them to help you run your business.

Chapter 13

How to Read Financial Statements

By David J. Lucier, CPA

Our experience shows that about 80 percent of our clients admit to not understanding how to read a financial statement when they become a client. Financial statements for publicly traded companies and large companies are usually very complex, requiring thousands of hours of studying in college and studying for the CPA exam in order to master the vast amount of rules and data. However, for most small businesses this process can be greatly simplified to allow the business owner to have the tools necessary to make the right decisions to run the business profitably.

There are two main financial statements that small businesses need to review on a monthly basis: the balance sheet and the income statement. These two documents will give most business owners the information needed to make good business decisions. First, the balance sheet will show an overview of the business.

Balance Sheet

The formula: Assets = Liabilities + Equity (A = L + E)

Definitions:
Assets: items of value. Example: inventory, company vehicles, cash accounts.

Liabilities: debts, amounts that you owe. Example: lines of credit, mortgage on business, vehicle loans.

Equity: capital (cash or assets) provided by the owner and profits increase equity. Losses and distributions decrease equity.

Balance sheet: a snapshot of the above formula at a point in time, usually the end of a month, quarter, or year.

Current assets: assets that will be converted to cash within one year. Example: cash, short-term investments, accounts receivables, and inventories.

Accounts receivable: when customers owe you money.

Accounts payable: when you owe suppliers money.

Inventory: property held for sale.

Sample Balance Sheet

XYZ Corporation
Balance Sheet
December 31, 2010

Assets

Current Assets
    Cash $10,000
    Accounts receivable   50,000
    Inventory   <u>70,000</u>
    Total Current Assets   <u>130,000</u>

Property and Equipment
    Land   50,000
    Building   100,000
    Machinery and equipment   <u>40,000</u>
        190,000
Less accumulated depreciation   <u>30,000</u>
        160,000

Other Assets   <u>30,000</u>
    Total Assets $320,000

Liabilities and Stockholders' Equity

Current Liabilities
    Notes payable $50,000
    Current portion of long-term debt   20,000
    Accounts payable   <u>70,000</u>
    Total Current Liabilities   140,000

Long-Term Debt   <u>110,000</u>
    Total Liabilities   <u>250,000</u>

Stockholders' Equity
    Common Stock   20,000
    Retained Earnings   <u>50,000</u>
        <u>70,000</u>

Total Liabilities and Stockholders' Equity $320,000

If the assets are greater than liabilities it gives a positive stockholder's equity. The larger the equity is the better for the company.

Income Statement

The Formula: Revenue (sales) − Expenses = Net Income (R − E = NI)

Definitions:
Revenue: results when a company sells services.

Sales: results when a company sells products.

Expenses: costs of producing revenue or sales, or costs of operating a business.

Net income: the bottom line.

Income statement (also called profit and loss statement, or P & L): statement of activity for a period of time, usually one month, multiple months, or a year.

Cost of goods sold: (Expense) represents the costs of producing goods for sale.

Gross profit: equals sales minus cost of goods sold (S − CGS = GP).

Operating expenses: a summary of expenses to operate a service business.

Selling, general, and administrative expenses: costs associated with management of business other than cost of goods sold.

Cash basis accounting: record expenses when paid and revenue when cash is received.

Accrual accounting: record expenses when incurred and revenue when earned.

Sample Income Statements

XYZ Corporation (Product Business)
Income Statement
For the Year Ended December 31, 2010

Sales	$500,000
Cost of goods sold (cost of sales) *	300,000
Gross Profit	200,000
Selling, general, and administrative expenses *	150,000
Income from operations	50,000
Interest expenses	30,000
Net income	$ 20,000

---

* These statements would normally involve detailed sub schedules.

RI Corporation (Service Business)
Income Statement
For the Year Ended December 31, 2010

Revenue	$500,000
Operating Expenses	
Payroll, officer	150,000
Payroll, other	160,000
Payroll taxes	28,000
Rent	12,000
Office expenses	20,000
Utilities	4,000
Insurance	8,000
Computer expenses	10,000
Telephone	3,000
Advertising	12,000
Travel and entertainment	13,000
Miscellaneous	30,000
Interest	30,000
	480,000
Net Income	$20,000

The larger the net income, the stronger the company is. In addition, net income as a percentage of sales is compared to industry averages and prior years.

Financial statements allow you to plan for future cash flow, taxes, budgeting, pricing studies, growth, borrowing needs, etc. They are the scorecard to evaluate the business performance. The above examples and explanations are the basics to understanding the balance sheet and income statement.

Budgets and Projections

In addition to financial statements, budgets and projections will help you manage your business. A budget is different from a cash flow, because a budget primarily looks at the income and expense of the business operations and does not include the cash that might come from investors or lending sources.

Budgets

Often originally prepared as part of a business plan, the budget allows a business owner to project the future income and expenses of the business. Although a budget can be prepared for a two-, five-, or even ten-year period, special attention should be given to creating and maintaining a budget for at least the next twelve to twenty-four months. By keeping a twelve- to twenty-four-month budget, the owners and management can more easily assess the business' ability to invest in a project or incur an unplanned expense. If a budget is not maintained, these decisions will need to be made without consideration of the financial impact to the business. It also is recommended that your budget be a working document that is reviewed and adjusted every six to twelve months. Because a budget not only addresses how income will be generated, but also estimates expenses, it can be a guide to hiring and can help to keep a business owner from hastily spending money by making the owners accountable.

Projections

Projections are financial forecasts that take your budget and make changes to the key components to determine what the best course of action might be for the business. The key components of a budget are sales, cost of sales, operation costs, and resulting profits or losses.

For example, a business might have a specific amount of financial resources to invest in a marketing plan. Therefore, to assess the best use of financial resources, the business owner might take the current budget and make modifications based on certain marketing options. After assessing the results of each marketing option, the option with the most efficient growth path might be selected as the best one. It might also be determined that the most successful growth plan is the least favorable path, because the business operations might suffer due to lack of qualified staff or other resource limitations that would be detrimental to the business' long-term success. Remember that rapid growth in many cases does not always lead to long-term business success. Business resources must always be monitored and evaluated in budgeting and evaluating projections.

Now that you have reviewed the financials, budgets, and projections, you can take a look at another crucial type of indicator: key operating statistics.

Chapter 14

Key Operating Statistics (Vitals)

By R. Sean Manning, CPA

After you've effectively compiled, used, and understood your balance sheet and income statement, the next step to managing your business is to use key operating statistics (vitals). These are numbers that can quickly show you that a potential problem might be developing, and they can be compiled on a daily, weekly, or monthly basis, much faster than the standard balance sheet and income statement reports.

There are many reasons a business begins to fail, and there are always signs that it is happening. If these signs start to present themselves, drastic changes may be necessary to save a struggling business. Too often the business owner measures success solely by cash flow. Although cash flow is important, cash flow is only one symptom of a business' success or failure.

Early Warning Signs of Trouble

Often there are early warning signs that lead to bigger cash flow problems when left unmanaged. A business owner should consistently monitor for warning signs, such as a declining customer base, a drop in average sale amounts, customer service complaints, or rising unplanned problems.

As consumers, we have all recognized businesses that appear to have lost an edge or are even showing early warning signs of decline and failure. Some examples might be a retailer that is carrying much less inventory than usual, an office or store that has become run down due to a lack of owner support, or even a restaurant or service company that never seems to have enough staff due to cuts they made to reduce costs. If you find yourself in this position, you should be very aware of your business perception, but also try to quickly access what your biggest challenges are and if they can be fixed.

If a business plan, growth plan, and budget were prepared, this is a good time to review them to see if any important facts were overlooked or not considered. With your new experiences as a business owner, you might now recognize key factors that could be missing from your original plans and budget. If it appears the plans and budget are still viable and attainable, a quick response to correct the oversight might be the only thing necessary to get the business going in the right direction. It might also be necessary for the business owner to solicit assistance from other professionals to evaluate the warning signs and offer advice on possible solutions. Just as important to fixing problems is recognizing that a problem may not be fixable and evaluating alternatives. Those alternatives unfortunately are often closure, bankruptcy, liquidation, and even sale of the business. These are obviously all challenging decisions, but they are important to consider if the business can't survive.

Key Operating Statistics (What Makes the Money)

It's important to monitor figures in your business that provides daily and weekly indicators of the business's success. Each business will have vitals that indicate their health. Much like a blood pressure reading or heart rate, these numbers will help you see how your money-making activities are working.

Although every business is unique, most can be categorized under a certain group or hold close resemblances to other businesses. These business groups have also studied important statistics that, if observed and managed, will provide a higher likelihood of success. You should have identified some key statistics or numbers that your business must monitor on a regular basis to help you manage and grow your company. Some examples of these might be:

- The number of patrons and average check total in the restaurant business
- Monthly sales per salesperson for a retail operation
- Hours billed per employee in a service business
- Manufacturing or job hours for a manufacturing or production business
- The amount of fabric needed to make a piece of clothing
- The packaging cost for a product
- The shelf life for raw goods meant for consumption

In addition to these statistics, you should also be reviewing your financial statements on a regular basis. Because the vitals do not appear on a business financial statement, it is important to establish a system to compile both pieces of information. It is recommended that both the vitals and accurate financial statements be compiled monthly for the business. Industry software can help a business compile vitals.

Often people put all their trust in periodic financial statements. Financial statements are an important part of business but often simply *confirm* that a problem exists rather than *indicate* that a problem exists. Additionally, many business owners rely on inaccurate and inconsistent financial statements. If you can't rely on the financial information, it could mask a problem. Masking a problem can lead to delays in discovering a problem and create even bigger issues associated with the problem. If you find yourself in a position of uncertainty with your business, seek advice from your advisers and look for manageable solutions to the uncertainty.

Accurate Financial Statements

Although some industry software or other off-the-shelf software might provide the ability to compile financial statements, it is important that the business owner finds a solution that will result in accurately compiled financial statements. There are a number of different affordable solutions that can assure that accurate financial statements are prepared and presented to the business owner. Affordable solutions would include hiring a qualified accountant, using an industry specialist, incorporating software solutions, and using technology tools to manage your financial statements. Important financial statements often include a balance sheet, income statement, and general ledger. A cash flow statement should also be considered based on the business owner's ability to interpret and use the cash flow statement.

When you have accurate financial statements and your moneymaking statistics, you should be able to accurately monitor the monthly production of the business. As you become more efficient with your monitoring, you can start to predict not only trends but also future income levels. With the ability to start predicting the future, we recommend updating your budget and your projections for at least the next two years to help manage the business.

Updating the Budget
With an updated budget, you can now not only see your income potential but also start to consider when and how you will need to invest money or additional resources into the business. One of the hardest aspects of owning and operating a business is trying to determine the right time to hire a new employee, invest in new equipment, and even expand to a new location. Too often

these decisions are never made, are made too late, or are even made prematurely. That is because sometimes these decisions are made based on available cash and not budgeted cash. When a budget is used, you can see when you might have the need for added resources, what cash might be available, and, if cash is not available, whether financing the new resource would be a better option. As you can see, having an understanding of your moneymaking statistics, preparing or investing in a good accountant that provides accurate financial statements regularly, and reviewing your budget should provide a greater opportunity for success.

Businesses Working Together

Now we would like to propose an idea that we feel is underutilized in the business world. It is a concept that many franchises use: share moneymaking statistics and financial statement information with your peers. This will help you to get accurate financial statements and give you a clearer picture of the overall market. Many business owners look at this concept as a threat. If you are in the printing business and you share your confidential information with the printer five miles away, it will affect your business. This is obviously a true statement, but the likely effect is that it will make you more efficient or even more profitable. Most of us can name numerous franchise businesses within blocks and certainly within miles of each other. Sometimes we see four or five similar franchises at the same intersection.

The truth is that if you work together with your peers, you most often become more knowledgeable, understanding, efficient, and even better at providing customer service. These traits will most likely drive business to you and add to your success. Most business owners don't belong to a franchise; therefore, it may be very important to become affiliated with a group of similar business owners or an association in an effort to meet and develop close business relationships with your peers. It is recommended that you search online for either a local or regional group that you can be a part of and encourage them to share statistical and financial information. Remember to meet and share this information with not only your peers but also your advisers at least once annually.

When you become knowledgeable on your own key operating statistics, you often develop a thirst to share your information and compare yourself to your peers. As a business grows and thrives, this thirst can become a vital part of maintaining the business' success. You will start to leverage your knowledge, which is why the next step in evaluating the business and your opportunities might lead you to do a deeper industry analysis and compare your business to the leaders in your industry.

Chapter 15

Key Operating Statistics (Vitals) Comparison to Industry Standards

By R. Sean Manning, CPA

Now that you've evaluated and understood your own business statistics, it might be time to start comparing your key operating statistics to others within your industry.

Although every industry has its own unique set of standards, most businesses can rely on some general formulas that are often utilized across all industries. Two of the most important are gross profit and break-even analysis.

Gross profit is defined as sales minus cost of goods sold. Mistakes are often made by not properly defining cost of goods sold.

Cost of goods sold is the direct cost attributable to the production of goods sold or service provided.

Break-even analysis is another important statistic to look at when starting and operating a business. A break-even analysis is a very sophisticated analysis that helps a business evaluate the varying components to determine what a business needs to do to break even and start to become profitable. The following is a list of terms that help define the break-even analysis.

Definitions Used in Break-Even Analysis
Fixed costs: costs that are required and generally do not change depending on increases and decreases of sales and or production—for example, rent expense. If you require office space, your rent expense will exist whether or not you have a sale that month.

Variable costs: costs that vary based on goods produced. An example would be tires on a car. The more cars you sell, the more tires you will need to buy, making it a variable cost based on the number of cars produced and sold.

Product sales: the number of items sold or service provided over a specific time period.

Item price: the amount paid for each item sold or service provided.

Break-even point: fixed cost / (unit selling price − unit variable cost)

Additional terms that may be useful when doing financial analysis are:

Total revenue: expected product sales times the item price for a specific time period.

Total cost: the sum of all fixed costs and variable costs for a specific time period.

Profit or (loss): total revenue minus total costs. Revenue in excess of costs results in a profit; costs in excess of revenue results in a loss.

Break-even analysis depends on the following variables:

- The fixed production costs for a product
- The variable production costs for a product
- The product's unit price
- The product's expected unit sales (sometimes called projected sales).

On the surface, break-even analysis is a tool to calculate at which sales volume the variable and fixed costs of producing your product will be recovered. Another way to look at it is that the break-even point is the point at which your product stops costing you money to produce and sell and starts to generate a profit for your company. You can also use break-even analysis to solve managerial problems such as:

- Setting price levels
- Targeting optimal variable/fixed-cost combinations
- Determining the financial attractiveness of different strategic options for your company

It is important to understand that break-even points can be very different based on the products and services being sold. For example, manufacturing, retail, and service businesses are all going to have a dramatically different break-even point, which is why it is so important to compare your business's break-even point with your industry once it is established.

Our website www.6stepstobusiness.com has a link to a break-even calculator that can be used to help you evaluate your own business.

Industry standards are the generally accepted statistics for a specific industry. They are often used to meet specific operational goals. Industry standards and guidelines are often created by analyzing successful businesses. It is then assumed that under similar conditions, other businesses will also be successful if they meet the industry standard. For example, an airline must fill a certain number of seats at a certain rate to make money on each flight, and a hotel must rent a certain number of rooms at a particular rate. Over time they become industry standards that are important to understand and compare to your business to be successful.

Industry standards can come from many places, but most often they are provided by trade associations or trade organizations, which is why it is recommended that business owners become active in their trade associations and organizations. For example, a veterinary office might choose to become a member of the American Veterinary Medical Association, and the owners of a glass installation business might find the National Glass Association very beneficial to their business.

If you have positioned yourself as a leader in your industry, you are probably seeing the benefits of being successful through healthy profits. And a healthy profit usually means tax planning opportunities. We'll review that in the next chapter.

Chapter 16

Tax Planning

By C. Gregory Orcutt, CPA

Nobody wants to pay taxes. However, if you are running a profitable business, you cannot avoid them. Paying as little as possible should be the goal, but also remember that no tax usually means no profit. There are many good tax-saving strategies that we would like to cover, but we will start with the ones that should be considered first.

Too many businesses pay too much tax because they have a bad accounting system. If your business does not account for every reasonable deduction, every penny spent and mile driven, you will miss the easiest tax deductions. So make sure you have a good accounting system in place with controls that assure that you do not miss any expenses or overstate your income.

Easy Tax Strategies

There are several financial changes that have a positive impact on your tax liability. Here are a few that every business owner should consider:

A **retirement plan** will allow a tax deduction without the cash leaving your hands. You will create a tax savings by moving money from one pocket to another. Any business, regardless of size and number of employees, can create a retirement plan that allows the owner and employees to defer income to later years. The owner will need to review the many types of plans that are reviewed later in this chapter to find the one that best meets their needs.

The amount of money contributed to the plan reduces the current year income and is invested tax deferred until retirement. If your company has employees, you will have to consider how much you want to fund their retirement accounts. Each plan has different employer contribution requirements that you will have to provide each year. You will want to work with a financial professional experienced in small-business retirement plans to choose the best plan for you and your employees. There may be a tax credit available for the start-up expenses of your retirement plan.

Purchased equipment can usually be fully deducted the year it is put into service. Normally when a fixed asset (furniture, computers, equipment, etc.) is purchased, it is depreciated over five to seven years. However, IRS code section 179 allows the cost of qualifying property to be fully depreciated in the year of purchase. There are limits as to how much can be purchased in a year, but careful planning can allow for a significant reduction in the taxable income. This type of purchase can be made up to the last day of the tax year and will still get a full deduction if the property is put in service before the year ends. So knowing your profitability throughout the year will allow you to make good investment decisions and avoid income tax.

Use an HSA for medical expenses. Medical expenses continue to rise in cost. The more of these costs that are paid with pretax dollars, the better. As a self-employed person, you are able to deduct the cost of your insurance premiums. However, most people spend a significant amount of money out of pocket that is not tax deductible. A health savings account (HSA)-qualified insurance plan will allow you to contribute to a savings account for your out-of-pocket medical expenses. You will get a tax deduction when the contribution is made. You do not need to spend the money to get the tax deduction; just put it in the savings account. The best part is that when you do spend the money, it is not taxable income. So, similar to an IRA, you get a tax deduction for contributing to the account, but if it is spent on medical care you never pay tax on the amount invested or on the growth. As an employer, you can also provide your employees with an IRS code section 125 plan, which will allow them to pay for their medical costs with pretax dollars. This will save you the FICA match on the amount they set aside in the plan. The type of entity the business is in will determine if the owner may participate in the 125 plan. Check with your business advisors when you establish your business entity to determine whether you can use this option.

Business Retirement Plans

One of the best tax-saving strategies for you and your business is to implement a retirement plan. Many business owners rely on the sale of the business to generate their retirement funding. Unfortunately, the sale of the business may not provide nearly enough money to live on for the rest of your life. A better strategy would be to fund your retirement each month so that you become financially diversified. If all of your investments are tied up in your business, you have all your eggs in one basket. If you have an established retirement plan, it gives you much greater flexibility when you start to negotiate the sale of your business. The sale will now supplement your retirement rather than being your only source for retirement. The other great benefit is that the money put into your retirement plan is tax deductible. This is one way to save taxes but keep the money in your own pocket.

The total allowable contributions in a year, including employee deferrals, are $49,000 per person (in 2011). If funding the maximum amount into your retirement plan is your goal, choosing the right plan is very important. The following is a summary of the plans you will want to consider.

A **simplified employee pension (SEP)** is the easiest plan to establish. The funding is done by the business and has to include any eligible employee. The maximum amount that can be contributed is approximately 20 percent of the self-employed owners' profits or 25 percent of any employees' wages. This plan works best for businesses without any employees. If the company has eligible employees, the percentage of contribution made for the owner has to also be provided to the employees. This can be an expensive plan if the owner intends to fully fund his own account.

An **individual 401(k) plan** is only available for a business that has no employees other than the owner and the owner's spouse. The plan has two funding components. The first component allows the owner to defer from his wages up to the maximum 401(k) plan limits, currently $16,500 (in 2011). The second is a company contribution of up to 25 percent of the owner wages. In order to maximize the annual limits of $49,000, the owner needs to have profits or a salary of $130,000, which allows a company contribution of $32,500 and salary deferral of $16,500. If you are over fifty years old, there is an additional allowed contribution of $5,000. This is an excellent plan if the business does not intend to have employees.

A **SIMPLE IRA plan** is for small businesses with less than one hundred employees. This plan has an employee deferral maximum of $11,500 and an additional $2,500 (in 2011) for those over fifty years old. The company must match dollar for dollar the first 3 percent an employee contributes or make a 2 percent contribution for all eligible employees. If employees do not participate in the plan, the owner is not disqualified from participating. This is a better option than a 401(k) for most small businesses, because if you do not have participation from your employees, the owner can still contribute to his account.

A **401(k) plan** is a much more complicated and expensive option compared to the others described. The maximum deferral allowed is $16,500 and an additional $5,000 (in 2011) for those over fifty years old. This plan requires annual testing and the preparation of a Form 5500 federal tax return each year. There is no required matching, but the employer may include that in their plan. If the owners want to contribute the maximum to their retirement plan each year, they must have a significant number of the non owners participate in the plan. If you want the higher deferral limits but do not have enough employees participating, then you can elect the safe harbor provision. This provision requires that the company match employee deferrals 100 percent for the first 3 percent, then 50 percent on the next 2 percent, or a contribution of 3 percent for all eligible employees. If the safe harbor is met, the owners can participate in the plan whether their employees participate or not.

The descriptions of each type of plan are very general and meant to give a basic overview of some of the options available. As an owner, you must decide how much you want to contribute yourself and also how generous you want to be to your employees. With that information, your financial professional will be able to help determine which plan is the best fit for your company. In my experience, a company without any employees will use the SEP or individual 401(k) plan. If you have or will soon have employees, the SIMPLE IRA or 401(k) with the safe harbor provision will be a good choice.

The investment decisions of the employees and company contributions should be the responsibility of the employee. You will want to work with a mutual fund company that has a variety of fund choices from which to pick. The fiduciary liability of making investment decisions for your employees is very high. You should put that responsibility in your employees' hands.

Taxes have to be paid, but there are basic strategies to utilize to minimize the amount. Although the exact figures and percentages for each type of retirement plan may change, the overall strategy remains the same—use proper tax planning to make better business decisions.

Chapter 17

Real Estate and Your Business

By R. Sean Manning, CPA

Most businesses require a physical location to operate and, therefore, the business will need to either lease property or consider buying property. For some business owners, the opportunity to own commercial real estate was never part of the plan, and for others it becomes the business owner's most valuable asset at retirement. For a new business the best solution is to look for property that is in a good location, functional for the business, and is offered at a reasonable rate. Most often the first step for a new business is to lease property rather than purchase. If this is the case, we recommend that the lease have some flexible terms, such as a month-to-month or annual renewal or a reasonable term of no more than two to five years.

Once the business is established and successful, the business owner may need to consider possible options and prepare for when the current real estate lease will expire. Many business owners choose to invest in the purchase of commercial real estate that is then leased to the business. Although we would recommend you consult with a commercial real estate agent if you are considering this option, we would also like to offer some information to consider if you are in the market for commercial real estate.

First, let's start with some questions you might need to consider:

How much is needed for a down payment? Typically a down payment for commercial real estate will be 20 percent of the purchase price.

Where do I get financing? Banks are typically the best resource for financing. They may partner with the Small Business Administration (SBA) and offer a loan secured in part or whole by SBA. Another option that is common is an owner-carried loan by the seller.

What are the loan terms? Most commercial loans are for twenty years or less. The interest rate can vary, but is usually closely related to the prime rate.

Start Planning Early

Consider contacting a commercial real estate agent months or even years in advance of your decision to buy commercial real estate. It is important that you start investigating options as early as possible to determine what types of properties are available and where the properties are located. You might determine early in your investigation process that the purchase of commercial real estate is not in your best interest.

Start Saving Now

Start building a savings sufficient for the down payment, and build a relationship with your banker so that he can be supportive of you when it is time to ask for financing.

Other Considerations

Consider what impact the move to a new location will have on your business. If your business requires a certain location to be successful, the option to purchase commercial real estate might be limited and/or price restrictive. If your business requires a specific location, consider asking your lessor if they are in a position to sell the commercial real estate. We also recommend that you ask for a first right of refusal when leasing from a third party to secure your right to purchase the property if the lessor decides to sell their commercial real estate.

However, if you can be flexible regarding your location, you will need to take a close look at how a new location might have an impact on your business. The new location might offer more visibility, a larger space, the ability to customize the space, and even better access for your customers, your staff, and your vendors. What will the cost of the move be, and how much will the maintenance of the commercial real estate be? Owning commercial real estate will have its advantages and disadvantages. Be sure to do a thorough evaluation of the property to determine the opportunities and the risks.

FIGURE 17.1: BUYING COMMERCIAL REAL ESTATE: ADVANTAGES AND DISADVANTAGES

Advantages	Disadvantages
Building equity	Property maintenance costs
Improvements that you own	Need to improve facility
Comfort of secure location	Less flexibility to move
Creating value for the future	Possible decrease in value
Expansion opportunity	Need for additional tenants

Buying commercial property is most similar to making an investment. Like investing you must evaluate your tolerance for risk and compare that to the opportunity cost and financial commitment to making this type of investment. This is a good time to consult with your advisers to get their opinion and help guide you to a decision with which you are comfortable.

Often the business owner will sell the business and retain the commercial property after the sale. This could not only provide a valuable asset to you in the future but also an income stream after the business is sold.

There are a number of tax considerations with commercial real estate. Please consult with your tax adviser regarding the possible tax implications. Most often a new limited liability company (LLC) is formed and used to buy the commercial real estate. There are often a number of reasons to avoid using a corporation or your business entity to purchase real estate. We recommend that you become familiar with the tax laws relating to passive activities and rental of real estate. Properly drafting a lease agreement is important, and consideration should be made in making the lease a triple net lease. Consult with your legal and tax advisers relating to the lease agreement. Another tax law you might want to become familiar with is the section 1031 exchange laws.

Owning and leasing commercial real estate to your business and/or another business could be very rewarding. Like all major decisions, do your research, discuss the option with your advisers, and consider all the advantages and disadvantages of commercial real estate ownership.

Once you've determined your real estate needs and implemented a plan, it might also be time to consider changes to your insurance. In the next chapter we will discuss real estate and other business-related insurances options for you to consider for your business.

CHAPTER 18

INSURANCE: A GENERAL OVERVIEW

By Lowell Lillge, CPA

Mention the word insurance and many people will instantly envision a monster company that is unwilling to pay out a dime when people need it. Whether that image is fair or not can be a topic of heated discussion. What I want to do here is give you a background on insurance and what it is supposed to do.

Insurance is the sharing of risk among a large number of participants in case a loss should occur. An early example of this is the Chinese traders who, in the third millennium BCE, put their products in many boats when they crossed dangerous waters. Their loss would be limited if one of the boats, which contained only a portion of their products, was lost rather than having all their wares on one boat. Babylonians, ancient Iranians, inhabitants of Rhodes, as well as Greeks and Romans also used various forms of insurance.

In the mid 1600s, over 13,000 houses were destroyed in a fire in London. This led to the creation of insurance, as we are familiar with it today. England's first insurance company was established around 1680 to insure homes. In 1732, the first insurance company was established in the American colonies in Charles Town (known as Charleston today), South Carolina.

As you know, the types of insurance have multiplied over the years. More than boats and houses are covered now. Other examples include health, life, renters, automobile, disability, product liability, and workers' compensation.

INSURANCE FEATURES

All types of insurance have the same basic features. Here are a few of the more common ones:

> **Amount of coverage:** When a covered loss occurs, what is the maximum amount the insurance company is obligated to pay? The loss, and subsequent payout by the company, may actually be less, but this is the maximum.
>
> **Exclusions:** What is it that is actually covered? For example, does the coverage include all medical expenses, or is dental excluded?
>
> **Premiums:** In order to have coverage an amount of money needs to be paid to the insurance company. The company then combines this money with premiums collected from other policyholders to cover the claims that it is obligated to pay.
>
> **Deductible:** This is the amount of the loss that the policyholder (you) must pay before the insurance kicks in. The deductible amount can vary depending upon your ability to absorb the loss yourself. The more you are willing to pay yourself (higher deductible), the lower your premiums will be. But, if you want the insurance company to absorb more, or all, of the loss your premiums will be higher.

A sudden event: Something must happen for the policyholder to incur a loss, and that event must be sudden (e.g., a bolt of lightning starts a house fire), not something that happens over a long period of time (e.g., rotting of the roof due to water seepage around the chimney).

Risk: Risk is the chance that something will happen.

Insurance is a promise that you will be made whole in case you suffer a loss. You are entering into a contract with the insurance company whereby it will reimburse you for a loss you might incur. In effect, you are betting you *will* have a loss, and the insurance company is betting you will *not*.

Personally, I hope the insurance company wins that bet.

BUSINESS INSURANCE

You've invested a lot in your business. Hopefully it has grown, or is growing, into a valuable asset for you. Certainly you want to keep it safe, right? That's where different types of insurance come into play. Here are a number of types of insurance you should consider for your business. Others may apply, but this is a starting point.

Business liability: This liability policy basically covers negligence of the business. The protection under this policy is made up of two parts. It will provide a legal defense if a lawsuit is started against your company, and it will pay the claim amount (up to the limits of the contract) if the suit is settled out of court or if a jury/judge awards damages.

Errors and omissions (E&O)/malpractice: If you provide services (e.g., legal or medical) and an event happens where you did not provide the appropriate services, or you made a mistake in providing them, you may be sued because you should have known that what you were doing was not right, or you should not have forgotten to do something. E&O or malpractice insurance covers you from these losses.

Workers' compensation (WC): WC insurance is meant to provide funds to a person who was hurt while working and is not able to perform any work at this particular time. It provides benefits while the employee is not able to work, and then it stops when the employee is able to return. Many states require employers to provide this for their employees and will penalize businesses if they don't.

Business interruption: What happens when your business is shut down due to a fire or some other disaster? Your customers cannot get into the store. If they can't get in, you can't make any sales. With no sales, you have no money coming in. However, you still have to pay the loan to the bank, the various insurance policy premiums, the telephone bill, and so on. Business interruption insurance is meant to cover these expenses. It provides funds you can use to pay these bills so that you can concentrate on getting the business operating again, rather than concentrating on how you're going to pay the bank.

Commercial auto: If you have automobiles in your business commercial auto insurance is necessary. It is similar to your personal auto insurance except that it covers the business. It provides collision, comprehensive, liability, medical, and uninsured coverage just as a personal policy does. Be sure that if the vehicle is owned by the business, the business (not you personally) is listed as the principal insured. You certainly don't want any confusion if there should be an accident.

Product liability: This is similar to the business liability except that it covers claims due to something your product has caused to happen.

Key person: What happens if the key person in your business, a fantastic sales rep or the one who handles most of the important daily operations, is unable to work due to illness, injury, or even death? How will the business avoid a traumatic impact on its financial operations? Is there a possibility it could even fail? Key person insurance is meant to prevent that. The benefits paid to the business can be used to pay the rent, the telephone bill, a loan, etc. This policy helps the business survive until the key person is able to return or is replaced. How much should the coverage be? You'll have to do some homework on that. Keep in mind how much in sales could be lost during that person's absence, how much it would cost to train the replacement, and other considerations your insurance agent discusses with you.

Buy/sell: A cousin to the key person insurance is buy/sell insurance. The basic purpose is so that if a partner dies, funds will be available for the other partner to buy the deceased's portion of the business. This assures continuation of the business rather than having to close it down. It can also be used by a single owner who enters into a buy/sell agreement with another business of the same type. The overall objective is the continuation of the business. Term life insurance is the most common vehicle used to fund the buy/sell agreement.

Health: This policy covers claims arising from medical and dental bills. It pays bills from doctors, hospitals, and clinics. Policyholders will pay the deductible, copayment, or coinsurance amounts, and then the insurance pays the rest, up to the limits of coverage. Health insurance is provided on an individual basis or on a group basis. When provided on an individual basis, a person pays the insurance company personally. Her premiums are based upon her current health status, her past medical history, and her direct family history. Group coverage is usually through an employer. Premiums can be fully paid by the employer or the employee can contribute a portion. Theoretically, premium rates are lower because there are more participants in the group; therefore, the insurance company is not putting all its eggs in one basket.

In summary, insurance is the sharing of risk among a number of parties that something unwanted will happen. If that unwanted event *does* happen, insurance is supposed to replace the economic loss. While we all hope we never have to make an insurance claim, it's best to have the coverage just in case. As the old adage says, "Better safe than sorry."

STEP 3:

HUMAN RESOURCES: THE PEOPLE FACTOR

Chapter 19

Assembling Your Team

By Lowell Lillge, CPA

To have a business rather than just a job, you will need people working for you. This chapter will help you find the right employees by thinking about the job itself, advertising for it, and hiring the best people.

Why Are Employees Necessary?

When you start your business, you have to do everything. But as the business grows, you won't be able to do everything. No one can do everything by himself for very long.

Even if you would *want* to do everything, you're not qualified. You can't be excellent at sales, production, planning, accounting, and taxes. You just can't. It takes different personalities to be successful at each of these disciplines. You don't have all those personalities. If you do, a trip to the psychiatrist might be in order.

So for your business to grow, you'll eventually need help. You'll need an employee, or two, or three, or more.

These employees can't just be warm bodies. The employees you hire should be people who are enthusiastic about your business and about working with you. They can make a big difference in the success (or failure) of your business, so they have to be committed to where you want the business to go.

Business Insight Technologies at www.hiringstrategies.com states that terminating an unproductive employee, or replacing your valued members who depart on their own, can cost one-half to five times a person's salary.[iv] So, how much is it worth to you to have the right person in the right job in the first place?

WHAT POSITION DO YOU WANT TO FILL?

One of the things you should have done by this point is to envision what you want your business to be. Through this vision process you will know what functions you want handled by employees.

Now is the time to determine which of those functions you want handled first. Which duties do you feel you can hand off to someone who will perform them as well as you (or perhaps even better)? Write down the specific job functions your new employee will handle.

Take your time here. Get specific. You want to be sure you know the type of job to be done so that you can concentrate on finding the right person.

Who is the right person for you? Do you know what qualities she will have? Think of the person who would be the perfect fit for you. What is her education? What is her experience? What are her personality characteristics (will you get along)? Write down everything, even if it seems to be pie in the sky.

When you have finished the list, review it to determine which qualities are most important—which qualities she *has* to have. Highlight them, and then concentrate on them during your selection process.

Assembling Your Team

Where Can You Find Good Employees?

Did you notice that we did not ask, "Where can you find employees?" We specifically stated *good* employees. That's what you want. You don't want someone who will fill up space. You want someone to help you grow your business!

So, where do you look? Many options exist:

- Help-wanted ads in the local newspapers
- State employment agencies
- Internet sites (e.g., Monster.com and CareerBuilder.com are two of the largest sites, but there are many others)
- Referrals from present employees
- Church bulletins
- Your business and social networks
- Local colleges or universities
- Chambers of Commerce
- Temporary personnel agencies and headhunters
- Industry and trade journals when looking for specialized positions
- Your company website
- Any other source you can think of

You want a large pool of good, qualified candidates. The more methods you utilize to search for good employees, the more good candidates you will have from which to choose. And the more good candidates you have, the more likely it is that you will find the perfect fit for you.

Making the Cut(s)

How are you going to start going through your applicants? Here are some suggestions to make the process easier and more productive.

THE APPLICANT'S FIRST CONTACT WITH YOU

How do you want the applicant to let you know of her interest in your job? Do you want her to send you a résumé, fax it to you, email it, or bring it in personally, or would you prefer that she call you? Do you require a résumé in the first place? Whatever your preferred method, be sure to spell it out in your ad.

Then, when the applicant makes that first contact, is it with your preferred method? If not, do *not* consider her any further. By not contacting you as you specified in the ad, she has shown that she cannot follow directions. If she cannot follow your directions now, she probably will find opportunities not to follow them in the future. Is that the kind of employee you want?

TESTING, INTERVIEWING, AND EVALUATING APPLICANTS

This brings us to the hard part—deciding who you want to work for you. Somehow you have to make a determination, and it has to be the right determination.

When people are starting a business they often know they will need to hire staff but don't always recognize that the biggest opportunity for a return on your investment comes from the people you hire.

Charlie Wonderlic, president of Wonderlic, Inc., says, "The single greatest return on investment comes from the people you hire, yet most companies spend more time evaluating a $10,000 copy machine than they spend evaluating potential employees.

The cost of not hiring the right people is the cost of mediocrity and failure. How much is that worth to you?"

Commit to putting in as much effort in to hiring and training your staff as you do for all the other important decisions you make for your business. Developing a system that brings the most qualified and the top performers to your company is critical.

There are three basic steps to this:

Testing

Are there minimum levels of proficiency (with measurable parameters) that are necessary for the position? Should the employee be prolific with mathematics? Does she need a license to fly solo in an airplane?

Determine what needs to be tested. Will you test her ability to learn, technical skills, people skills, intelligence, integrity, reliability, math knowledge, or something else? Devise or obtain tests to measure her proficiency in the required areas. Determine what acceptable scores will be.

In administering the test to the applicants, consider whether they should take the test individually or whether you can give the test to a number of people at the same time, in the same room. Giving the test to a group can save you time in the long run.

When the testing is done, grade each applicant. Divide the graded tests into three groups: good, average, and below average. You do not want to talk to the below-average applicants. Keep the average applicants for possible further consideration. Then set times to talk with the above-average individuals.

Interviewing

When you talk to an applicant, you expect him to be prepared for the interview. After all, why wouldn't he come prepared? He's looking for a job, isn't he?

The applicant, on the other hand, is also expecting you to be prepared. After all, why wouldn't you be prepared? You're looking for a good employee, aren't you?

Hold yourself to the same standard you expect from your applicants. You want to make a good impression on a good candidate. Finding, training, and retaining a good employee is a major investment you're making in your business. Therefore, be prepared before he walks in.

During the interview, ask open-ended questions—questions that ask who, how, what, where, when, and why. "Tell me about ..." is also a good way to get an applicant to talk about things. Remember, you're looking to get information about the applicant, and the way to do that is to get him talking. A question that can be answered with yes or no will not get him talking.

Here are a few questions that should get the applicant talking:

A. *What is the best thing about your current (or your most recent) job?* You want someone who can give you a thoughtful answer because it means she can actually think, rather than just handle the rudimentary technicalities of the job.
B. *Why are you leaving your current position?* Watch out for someone who criticizes his present employer.
C. *What was the toughest problem you faced in any of your jobs? How did you overcome it?* You need to know how the applicant handles situations that don't go strictly according to plan.
D. *What improvements did you make in your last job? What improvements would you have liked to make?* This gives you a look at the applicant's creativity.
E. *What has been your most interesting job so far? Why?* The reasons for this answer are more important than the answer itself.
F. *Tell me about the best coworker or supervisor you've had.* Again, you're looking for reasons.
G. *What kind of people rub you the wrong way? What annoys you?* This gives you an idea of how the applicant will fit within your company.
H. *If you decide to start working with us, how would you like us to assist you?* Look for balance. You don't want an applicant who indicates he needs a lot of help. You also don't want an applicant who says he probably won't need much, if any, help.

When you're done with the interview, end it. That may sound trite, but some interviews go on, and on, and on. Get the information you need to make a sound decision, and then go to the next step.

Evaluating
Now that you've talked with the candidates you thought could be good, it's time to evaluate them and select one.

After each interview, summarize all the information you received about the applicant. Write it down so you can refer to it later. It has to be written because you'll never remember everything about each applicant after you've talked to a few, unless it is written down. Your memory just isn't that good.

Look over the answers you received and the notes you took during the interview. How does he fit into your organization? He should be good—no, very good—or don't consider him any further. Remember, you're looking for *good* (preferably great) employees.

There are a few other things you may want to use in your evaluation before you make your choice.

Michael Mercer, Ph.D., author of the book *Hire the Best & Avoid the Rest* recommends "9 Unique and Amazingly Useful Ways to Evaluate Job Applicants."[v]

Reference Checks

Are these really necessary, or are they just a waste of time? You're only going to get good references anyway, aren't you? The answer is that you must check references thoroughly, just to be sure the applicant is not blowing hot air. To be sure the references are checked thoroughly, *you* should check them yourself. Don't abdicate that job to someone else.

1. *Start checking references right away.* The longer you wait the more chance you have of losing the applicant.

2. *Take letters of reference given to you by the applicant with a grain of salt.* They may have been written by the former employers to help themselves feel better about letting the person go.
3. *Call to get references. Do not send reference requests by mail.* This gives you the opportunity to evaluate whether the voice on the other end of the phone line sounds truthful or not. Also, you just might get a more candid evaluation, because nothing is being written down by the former employer.
4. *Talk to other references not mentioned by the candidate.* Call his previous employer and ask to talk to someone else who knew the applicant. Ask that person who else you should/could talk to about the applicant, and so on. You want to be sure you are comfortable with the background of your future employee.
5. *Call most of the applicant's former employers.* Maybe the most recent employer thought he was the model employee, but without checking, you will never know what employers before that one thought of him.
6. *If the former employer gives you a good reference, ask whether he would rehire the applicant if given the chance.* If he wouldn't, why not? When someone gives an employee a good reference, yet does not want him back, this should make you think that the former employer is not telling you everything you need to know. Dig deeper. You need to know exactly what the former employer is keeping from you.
7. *If the position is important enough, personally visit the person to get the reference.* You just might get a more candid conversation about the applicant. (Besides, this gives you the opportunity to evaluate the body language of the reference to see if he's comfortable with what he's telling you.)

Marketing Your Business to the Applicant

You've gone through a lot of time and effort to finally decide upon the person who is going to be a great addition to your business. But you're not done, yet.

You've found the right person for you, but now you have to get your prospective employee to *want* to work with you.

The more of the following that you can offer, the more attractive your company will be to your new employee:

- Personally rewarding work
- A well-thought-out job design
- Reasonable job demands
- A safe and healthy work environment
- Employee–supervisor relationships that are positive
- Competitive wages and benefits
- Training
- Employee development opportunities
- Management that listens to employees and considers their input
- Job security

Make the Offer and Get the Employment Contract

What remains now is to go get the employee.

Call the applicant as soon as you have made your decision. You don't want to lose him to someone else! Grin from ear to ear. Let him hear how excited you are so he knows how much you want him by your side.

By the end of your selection process, you should know his time frame. Tell him when you'd like him to come in to start work. Tell him about the wage and benefit package (minute details can be left for when he comes in).

When he comes in, have the employment contract ready for him to sign. This lays out what you expect of him and what he can expect of you. Be sure you have the employment contract either written or reviewed by your attorney.

We've briefly mentioned wages and benefits, a very important consideration for employees. The next chapter will delve into this in more detail.

Chapter 20

Compensation and Benefits

By C. Gregory Orcutt, CPA

As mentioned in the previous chapter, you want to hire the right person for the job, so compensation and benefits are crucial factors in attracting employees. Here are some considerations to keep in mind when making these decisions.

One of the biggest decisions an owner makes is when to hire the first employee. It can be difficult to determine when there is enough work to keep someone else busy for forty hours a week. There is also the concern of how much you can pay them without causing a hardship. There are a lot of financial and emotional issues behind this decision. But without employees, an owner will not be able to grow the business.

Some key indicators that an employee might be needed are if you are falling behind in invoicing your customers, bookkeeping, bank reconciliations, ordering material, returning phone calls, or the completion of customer work. Or maybe the owner is working too many hours, spending too much time on clerical responsibilities, or not following up on sales opportunities. If any of these problems are occurring, you need to consider getting help. If you don't you can hurt the value of your business and risk losing it.

Once you decide to grow your business by hiring more help, you must decide how much to pay, how often, and what benefits to offer. Some decisions may be established by federal or state minimum wage laws, union agreements, or industry standards.

Employees can be compensated many ways. Often the pay type is determined by their grade of work. For instance, most production, construction, retail, and office administration workers would be paid on an hourly basis. The more responsibility employees have, the more likely they will be compensated with a salary. Employees that can be provided an incentive may have a combination of commission and salary. Often the industry you work in will have standards that employers have used for years. To be competitive you will have to follow those standards. The following are the typical pay types you will select from.

Pay Types:

- Hourly: pay rate that is paid for each hour worked
- Salary: pay rate that is the same each pay period; usually assume the same number of hours worked each pay period
- Commission: a percentage of a performance measurement; often salespeople are paid a percentage of the sales they produce
- Overtime: often required by law; pays one and a half times an employee's normal hourly rate for time worked over forty hours a week

Benefits:

The cost of hiring an employee can be much more than the wage he receives. Often a business owner will want to provide other benefits to his employees. The decision the owner must make is how much money the business will contribute versus what the employee will pay. There are many state and federal guidelines that regulate what benefits must be provided. Often that is determined by the number of employees a business has. Due to the quickly changing regulations and differences of each state, we will not list these regulations, but you will need to consult a professional to confirm you are in compliance with the labor laws in your state.

Determining which benefits to offer your employees can be difficult. You want to be generous; however the cost can be significant. As mentioned above, some benefits will be mandated by federal or state law. You will need to understand what might be required of your business. Often the owner has to decide which benefits will be provided and which employees will be eligible. A human resources professional can help you sort out all the options. But many businesses that are hiring their first employee have to start with what they can afford. The following are typical benefit plans you can offer:

- Sick pay: normal wages paid for days the employee is sick. Usually the number of days is limited.
- Vacation pay: pay for time away from work; usually time paid increases with years of service.
- Family leave: paid or not paid time off for extended absences related to family issues. The employee's job is maintained during the absence.
- Insurance: can provide health, disability, or dental insurance. Employer can provide full benefits or require the employee to share in the cost through payroll withholding.
- Retirement plan: allows employee to defer income into an investment account, which reduces their taxable income. Employer may match employees' contributions or contribute company funds to their account.
- Cafeteria plan: allows employee to pay for benefits with pretax dollars. Often the employee portion of

health insurance and medical flexible spending plans are a part of this plan.

Compensation for employees can include both wages and benefits. By making a wise choice of what to offer your staff, you'll gain their respect and loyalty. In the next chapter, we'll discuss how training your employees is crucial to your success.

Chapter 21

Training Employees

By C. Gregory Orcutt, CPA

Business owners often struggle to find the time to manage all the aspects of running their business. They never feel like they have the time to get to every project on their list. Helping their employees become the best they can be at their job is one area business owners tend to ignore. As owners, we know we need to find people to help us grow our business. But no one is skilled enough to do all that we need without training. Many times our employees are growing up in the business as we have. They were never trained to perform all the tasks they are asked to do.

So how do we move everyone in the organization to be better at what they do? How much should be spent to train our employees? There are many books and consultants that you can use to create your employee training program. But here are some basic concepts to help you implement some changes in your organization.

Create Job Descriptions

If you don't know what your employees' roles are, how can you provide training? Put on paper the role they play and the processes they manage or are a part of. Interview your employees and make sure you understand all their responsibilities. You should also document how each employee's work is generated. For instance, the salesclerk entering a sales order receives that sales order from the salesperson. The clerk's job description will document that what he enters originates from the salesperson, and the salesperson's job description will document his responsibility to provide the salesclerk with the order. This way everyone understands how work flows through the company and what is expected before and after someone completes his task.

Identify Skill Sets
What types of skills do they use now—technical, relational, physical, and any others? What types of tools are they using? What software do they spend most of their time using? What kind of interaction with people do they have—on the phone, in person, on the computer? All the skills each employee needs should be documented.

Prioritize Skills Needed Company-Wide
Make a list of all the skills identified above. Then prioritize them by how many hours are spent using that skill throughout the company. If everyone uses a particular computer program daily, then mastery of that program may be a top priority. The list should include skills that are needed by everyone in the business, including the owner. It should also include time-management and relational skills. A good example would be if everyone uses Microsoft Outlook®. Chances are that everyone is not using that program to the fullest and as efficiently as it could be. Spending an hour in a company-wide training program could save many more hours in the future and ensure everyone is using all the features in the same way.

Identify Who Can Teach the Skill
Start with the number-one priority and find the best source for strengthening that skill. If it is a software program, find out

if the software provider has a trainer or identify the best user within your company. Most people will learn better from someone outside the company rather than an insider. Go through every priority on the list and find the best resource to increase everyone's level of skill.

Create a Timetable and Budget

This is not a process that can be done quickly. If training is something that has been neglected, then start small. If you are just getting started in your business, then create an ongoing program of training and make it an essential part of your culture. If you can improve on a skill that the majority needs, the productivity gain will be noticeable. Create a day of the month that some element of training is provided. Stick to it! Don't let the busy times get in the way.

Evaluate and Celebrate Your Wins

Get feedback from your employees so that you know what kind of training is making your team more productive and valuable. You can also confirm with your customers that they notice a difference. Celebrate the difference you are seeing within your business. Encourage your employees to put into practice what they are learning. You might need to provide some incentives to try something new. Training is just the start. People will not implement change that is uncomfortable. It will take time to get over the discomfort of the change. But it will be worth it in the long run.

The goal should be an ongoing process of training and improvement. There are not many businesses that remain the same forever. The work our customers pay us to do is constantly changing. The business that is successful over the long haul is one that adapts to this change. This process is always true for the owner. You should be reading the many books available on growing and improving your business. There are seminars that can keep you up to date on the current trends in your industry. Don't stop learning.

Once you've invested in hiring an employee, continue to improve your investment with clear and thorough training for staffers. This is an investment that will pay off in the future.

Once trained, staffers will need feedback. The next chapter focuses on evaluating and coaching your employees.

Chapter 22

Managing Staff

By C. Gregory Orcutt, CPA

The team of employees that surrounds you is going to be the reason for much of your success and for much of any failure in your business. They will be the face of a growing company and allow you to leverage your time. Your time will be much more productive as you allow your team to perform the tasks you do not like doing or are not good at doing.

How can you create a team that will work hard to help you grow your business? What are the important factors in creating a great team?

In most small businesses the owner will be managing the employees. You will be doing the hiring, training, evaluating, and firing. For most of us, this job does not come naturally. Until your business is large enough to afford a human resources manager, it is up to you. You might think doing most of the work yourself would be easier, but that would be a huge mistake. You need a team of people that will perform the skills and functions that you do not do well. You will also quickly learn that, to grow the revenue and profits of the business, you need their help.

In his book *Good to Great: Why Some Companies Make the Leap... and Others Don't*, author Jim Collins discusses the concept of "getting the right people on the bus." Too often we settle for the first person to respond to our help-wanted ad. Collins says, when in "doubt, don't hire—keep looking. Of course this means that a company should limit its growth based upon its ability to attract enough of the right people."[vi] A quick test to determine whether you have the right person after he has been hired is to ask: If you had known when you hired the employee all that you do now, would you hire him again? If you would not hire him again, he is not the right person.

Often rather than kicking employees off the bus, they need to be moved to a different seat on the bus. Many times employees are in the wrong position in the company. They may be exactly the kind of people you want but you need to find a better-fitting role for them. In a small company it can be difficult to create new positions. But making the changes to align a good employee with the right job can open the door to a great long-term employee relationship.

Motivation: Yours and Your Employees':

Understanding what motivates each of your employees is necessary for creating a great team. Everyone is motivated by something different. Follow these steps to create a better environment for motivating your employees.

1. First understand what motivates you. Your employees will follow your example. If you are excited about your job, others will be too. But if you always have a negative attitude, don't expect those around you to feel any better about their job.
2. Find out what motivates each of your employees. They want to enjoy their job, so ask them to share with you

what motivates them, and observe when they appear to enjoy their work and when they really do not want to be there. The more background you have on your employees, the better you can help them enjoy their job. You may find that an employee has writing skills and would love to write the company newsletter. Or someone has a green thumb and would enjoy creating an outdoor lunch area. This could also lead to some cost savings if outsourced projects could be done by your employees, while at the same time it could lead to greater job satisfaction. Make a list of what motivates each employee. Everyone's list will not be the same. Ask their coworkers or managers what they have observed. You can use this information to create goals and the appropriate rewards that will be unique for each employee.

3. Do not assume that your employees' paycheck is the only reason they come to work. Yes, you need to be competitive and have the appropriate benefits, but each of your employees will respond differently to financial rewards.

4. Share with your employees the feedback you received from your customers or other employees, good and bad. They need to understand that their actions can have a lasting effect on the success of the business. Many employees will find great satisfaction from a customer's comment. You must find ways to garner customer feedback if it does not come easily.

5. One bad employee will ruin good employees' motivation. As business owners we should be slow to hire and quick to fire. However, we often do just the opposite. Don't let the bad apple ruin the rest. If someone should not have been hired, do not waste time; fire them. Employee morale and motivation will increase instantly.

6. As the business owner, you have to be the best encourager you can be. It might not be your personality to be an encouraging person. But we can all improve in this area. Start now by saying something positive to an employee each day. The more you do it, the easier it becomes. This attitude will spread to others, but it will start with you.

Your Company's Culture and Effects:

Your company will need to work hard to develop a trusting environment in your organization. Developing your people skills may be the best investment you can make. We tend to put our emphasis on sales and production training; however, if people don't like working in your company, they will not perform well. Consider the following results from the Gallup Organization's study of 3 million employees across 300,000 work units in corporations:[vii]

(29%) Engaged employees work with passion and feel a profound connection to their company. They drive innovation and move the organization forward.

(54%) Not-engaged employees are essentially checked out. They are sleepwalking through their workday, putting in time—but not energy or passion—for their work.

(17%) Actively disengaged employees aren't just unhappy at work; they are busy acting out their unhappiness. Every day, these workers undermine what their engaged coworkers accomplish.

If you think that working on your company culture is a waste of time, I recommend familiarizing yourself with the work of John Kotter and James Heskett,[viii] both of whom are retired professors from Harvard Business School. Their research shows that improving your corporate culture improves your bottom line. Finding the time to work on the operations and culture of your company versus its growth and gaining customers can be a challenge. But to give your company the best chance of success, you must invest some time to developing your corporate culture. You might also find that you enjoy going to work more yourself.

Chapter 23

Terminating Staff

By Lowell Lillge, CPA

In the previous chapter, we discussed managing your staff and giving them feedback, among other things. These are designed to develop the employee into a valuable and productive member of your team.

There might be times, however, when the best hiring procedures, compensation, benefits, training, supervision, and management just won't get you the employee you need. After all this, when you have an employee who isn't working out your best decision may be to terminate his employment. This chapter will help you determine how to handle that situation.

Why Is the Termination Necessary?

Unless you are releasing the employee because of a specific occurrence (e.g., drinking on the job, sexual harassment) the case against the employee should have been building for a while. There are good reasons he can no longer remain with your business.

As time progressed, you should have been keeping notes on the lack of progress of the employee. These notes will detail what the problems have been, what the corrective action is that you and the employee have agreed to, and the (lack of) results since that agreement. Be sure to document everything. You never know when, or if, you will have to substantiate your actions in a court of law.

Steps in the Termination Process:

1. The termination meeting should be handled by the employee's immediate supervisor. An observer should also be in attendance to attest to what happens in the meeting just in case the employee alleges, later, that something discriminatory happened during the meeting. It would be good if the observer was someone of the opposite sex from the supervisor. An observer will also provide a calming effect to help curb emotions from getting out of control.
2. Get organized. Know what you are going to say. Write the reasons for the termination, and have them with you for the meeting with the employee.
3. Bring the employee into your office. State directly that he is being terminated and why. Don't try to lighten the situation with small talk or jokes beforehand. Stick to the facts. Thank him for his service and wish him the best in his future efforts.
4. Have all payments due the employee ready. Give him any benefits that are due. You want to be sure that he will not be feeling you are holding back on anything that is due him. That could lead to a lawsuit.
5. Have the employee relinquish all company property that may be in his possession (e.g., cell phone, keys to a company car). Have him give you any and all passwords he may have that are necessary to operation of company computers.

6. Give the employee time to gather his personal effects from his work area (about thirty minutes should be sufficient). It is permissible for you to accompany him during this period.

OTHER CONSIDERATIONS IN THE TERMINATION PROCESS

1. Do not fire an employee when you are angry. Practice self-control. If an event happens that is so far out of the realm of acceptable company policy, consider suspending the employee. Then you can cool down and determine whether firing him is the correct thing to do or if some other disciplinary action should be taken instead.
2. Follow any and all written company policies.
3. Do it in person. While it may be easier to handle this via telephone or e-mail, give the employee some respect by having the meeting face-to-face.
4. Don't make the session any longer than it needs to be. That will just make things harder for you and the employee.
5. Use tact, a lot of tact, an awful lot of tact. Give him a good, truthful explanation that he can live with.
6. If the employee tries to argue with you or lashes out at you, politely listen. Let him vent. Do not argue back. Do not show him how right you are (you will always be wrong in his eyes, anyway). After he's finished, continue on with the termination in a professional manner.
7. Watch what you say to others. Tell them the employee will no longer be working in your company. No explanation is necessary to others. Don't deride or degrade the ex-employee. That could make other employees wonder how you talk about them behind their back. You want to keep your integrity intact.

8. Conventional wisdom holds that the best time to terminate an employee is early in the day, early in the week. This gives him the rest of the week to start his search for a new position rather than giving him two or three days (the weekend) to let the termination fester before he can start looking.

SELF-EVALUATION

After the dismissal, sit down and take a hard look at why this employment opportunity failed. It is now your time to determine what went wrong so that changes can be made to ensure a situation like this won't (or is less likely to) happen in the future.

Look at every detail of the employment experience and ask questions:

1. Did you advertise in the right places to get enough qualified applicants?
2. Was your testing procedure adequate?
3. Did you get everything out of the interviews that you could have?
4. Did the employee fully understand what would be required of him?
5. Was the training adequate?
6. How was your supervision?
7. Why couldn't the employee perform up to requirements?

These are starting questions in your self-evaluation. Think of others. Use them all to determine why the termination was necessary. Then make the appropriate changes before you start looking for your replacement.

CASE STUDY: MARK

The information here is not just a scholarly dissertation; it's based on the experience of one of our clients in terminating employees. Here is an example:

Our client needed someone for his Accounts Payable (AP) department. He ran ads in the local newspapers, in the large metropolitan newspaper, with the county unemployment office and on the bulletin board of the local technical school.

Many resumes came in. Most of them were dismissed right away because the applicants were unqualified. He called a few with some preliminary questions and invited a few of those to come to the office for further conversations. Mark (not his real name) was one who came in.

His test results were just a bit out of the parameters the employer would have considered to be acceptable. However, his educational degree was such that he thought it might have just been test-taking jitters. So he interviewed Mark.

The interview was like so many others that he had conducted over the years-nothing tremendous, but nothing awful, either. He was impressed with what seemed to be Mark's strong desire to work hard. He conducted another interview a few days later and came away with the same feeling-nothing tremendous, but nothing awful, either.

He needed someone in the AP department and he knew he could train Mark for the job, so he offered it to Mark and Mark accepted. Our client felt good because his slot was filled.

After the initial orientation to the office and the business, he set about training Mark. He knew it would take time, maybe six to twelve months, before Mark would be able to function completely on his own. That was okay.

After six months, Mark was still in need of training. He wasn't grasping some of the fundamentals of the job. His supervisor had to go over everything he did to be sure it was accurate. That's the way it is with training, though. You have to check to be sure the employee is learning.

Mark tried hard, though. He really tried hard. There are few employees who have the dedication that Mark had. Our client was impressed by how hardworking he was.

Twelve months into the training, Mark understood a little more, but his supervisor still had to check everything he was doing. In effect, the supervisor was redoing everything Mark did to be sure it was accurate.

During this year, the supervisor was training him (sit-down, hands-on training) and giving him feedback.

Eighteen months passed and the situation had not improved. It was still taking two people to do the job one should have been handling. Plus, our client wanted Mark to handle more than he had at that specific time. So, he had two people doing less work than he wanted one person to do.

He started keeping notes on what problems were occurring, what mistakes were being made repeatedly, what training procedures were being undertaken, what objectives were to be reached within specific timeframes, and what the results were.

Between the eighteenth month and the twenty-fourth month, he started thinking he had made a bad hire. What in the world took him so long to realize that? But…

Mark tried hard. He really tried hard. How could he let someone go who was so loyal and tried so hard?

By the thirtieth month, nothing had changed. Nothing. Our client finally accepted the fact that a change had to be made. If nothing else, he just had to let Mark go. With his supervisor doing the same job, he would at least be saving Mark's salary.

Over one specific weekend, he decided that the next Friday morning he would let him go. What an anguishing week that was! Our client knew what was coming, but Mark didn't. Friday morning he arrived at the office before Mark. No one else would be coming in that day. Vacations had been previously arranged.

Perfect. No one else would be around to witness what was going to happen. That would make it easier on Mark.

Terminating Staff

As soon as he came in, Mark was called into the office. Our client went over his accomplishments and failures. He reviewed what remedial steps had been taken over the past two and a half years to get him trained and fully functioning. He stated that he appreciated his loyalty to the company and that he was such a hard worker. He stated that, although he tried so hard, Mark wasn't performing up to the standards required for the position.

He then stated that he had to let him go. A payroll check was ready for him, along with a check for four weeks' severance pay. He then asked Mark to get his personal effects from his workstation and turn in his office key on the way out.

Mark started collecting unemployment compensation (UC) payments right away. The client's UC rate went up for a while, but that was fine. He considered it a small price to pay for a larger mistake.

About four or five years later, our client received a call from Mark. He needed some information regarding a business client they had in common. In that time, he had found a position with a company, and at the time he called, Mark said that he was now a partner in that company.

Things worked out well for Mark. Things worked out well for our client.

Now, considering what we went over earlier in this chapter, can you tell how many things our client did wrong? Did he do anything right? What could have been improved? How?

You can be sure of this: His self-evaluation has been deep, comprehensive, and ruthless. He has learned from this. He has told me that a situation like this will never happen again!

That's what your self-evaluation must produce.

If you must terminate an employee, be sure to follow standard steps in doing so, be as considerate as possible during the process, and perform a self-evaluation to learn from the experience.

STEP 4:

OPERATIONS: WORK FLOW, CUSTOMERS, AND SALES

Chapter 24

Managing Daily Operations

By R. Sean Manning, CPA

Often something as simple as a systematic approach to doing something can give a business a competitive edge. When you also add committed qualified staff to the equation, along with an organized management team, the result can be a very successful business.

On the other hand, especially during the early stages of starting and running a business, owners can start to feel overwhelmed and might consider taking shortcuts. When business owners become overwhelmed, they become reactive rather than proactive. You might spend more time putting out fires than planning to avoid fires in the first place. Avoid taking shortcuts to run your company.

Develop Operating Systems

To avoid shortcuts proper planning, monitoring company systems, studying the competition, and developing new strategies should all remain important to the business owner. Do not let these functions become overshadowed by the day-to-day activities and challenges that you will be faced with. Here are some steps to take:

ADAPT AND EXPLORE NEW EFFICIENCIES

When the business is running well, consider exploring opportunities to become more efficient. Look at your business from the customers' or employees' perspective. You might uncover weaknesses that need to be fixed. Being efficient starts with some simple steps, like having napkins in the napkin dispenser if your business is a restaurant. The challenge now is what system to have in place to make sure the napkins are always in the dispenser. When you don't have to worry about the napkins being in the dispenser, you can focus on ways to work smarter and provide better products and services.

DEVELOP SYSTEMS AND CONSISTENCY

Similarly to franchises, all business owners should find a systematic approach to their business operations that allows for consistency. Your customers and/or clients will expect consistency in your product or service. To meet consistency expectations, you must use a systematic approach. This systematic approach not only gives you the tools to meet expectations but also allows you to train and manage your staff effectively. Once you and your staff are trained and working efficiently, you must also develop a way of measuring your success. A consistent system is more easily managed and evaluated. Consistency also allows a business owner to consider growth and to grow more effectively. Most businesses thrive on being unique and great at one thing rather than average or good at many things. Consider how you will be different, and search for ways that can give your operation a competitive edge.

IMPLEMENT TRAINING: OWNER AND STAFF

A properly defined system will help the business owner define ideal employee characteristics. Those employee characteristics can then be used to interview and test potential staff during the hiring process. An efficient hiring process helps lead to an easier and more efficient training process. When employees are in jobs they like and understand, they are more committed and better serve your customers and clients. After you have a well-managed business and are doing well at meeting the needs of your customers, don't rest on your success. Look for ways to improve the skills of yourself and your staff. This will allow your business to maintain a competitive edge.

Manage the Marketing

The business plan may have also laid the framework of a marketing plan. Without customers and a way to maintain and acquire new customers, no business will last long. Thinking outside the box when preparing and reviewing a marketing plan can lead to some very fun and successful growth opportunities. Combining unique marketing techniques along with using the traditional marketing techniques for your industry can set your business apart from others. This is another way that resting on your success can lead to problems within your business. Continue to manage and build a marketing plan that keeps your customers happy and new ones coming in the door.

Practice Good Customer Service

We have all heard the phrase in real estate: location, location, location. In business it is all about the customer, and we should be thinking *customer service, customer service, customer service.* It makes me very happy to see people doing the job that they love. They generally are so happy and dedicated to their job that customers want to buy their product or service and work with them. On the other hand, we have all seen people and owners doing something that they appear to be working hard at. When you consider a business opportunity, ask yourself if you are passionate about that business. If you are, customer service is easy. When customer service is easy, you become very good at servicing customers and you will build a loyal customer base. A loyal customer base is the foundation of a successful, well-maintained business. Your staff will also adapt your passion and allow you to build a rewarding business for yourself and a rewarding career for them.

Systems are a part of everything you do when you own and operate a business. We talked about systems and consistency, training staff, marketing, and customer service. Be creative and look ahead to the future of your business. Every day you go to work, you have an opportunity to evaluate and improve your business. Take some time every day to find something you want to do to make you business better—simple things like giving employees encouragement and additional training that will make them better employees. It's the little things that add up and put you in a position to also incorporate bigger projects and grow your business.

What If the Business Is Not Meeting Expectations?

As much as any business can plan, there is often a point when a business owner will make one of two realizations. Unfortunately for many, one realization is that the owner feels disappointed in their lack of success and opportunity, and although it is difficult to discuss, the business must to be closed, dissolved or liquidated. Studies have shown and logic would support the hardest years for a business to be successful are the first 5 years. General business circumstance along with other outside or personal challenges are constantly at play and affect the success of the business.

Business owners who decide to close their business must not only face the frustration of dealing with closing their business but also the possible financial, legal, and personal challenges as well. It is important to recognize the signs, take action and be willing to make good decisions to avoid having your business destroy other aspects of your life. Some of these signs might include a drop in cash flow, lower customer count, higher operational costs, employee turnover, and longer work hours for the owner. As excited as you might be about starting your business, also promise yourself that if the business is failing you will take the proper steps to close and dissolve the business to avoid other possible personal failures that can be triggered by closing a business improperly.

Fortunately, there are many businesses that become successful not only for themselves, but also for their staff and their families. These business owners have leveraged what they have learned, applied basic fundamentals, and often moved into an ownership position that starts to change from survival to comfort and gratification. When that happens, the business owner might shift focus from systems management to customer service and other areas that allow the business to expand through increased marketing and sales.

Chapter 25

Managing Customers: Credit, Collections, and Service

By David J. Lucier, CPA

Managing customer credit and finance is comprised of three main areas: establishing credit policies and procedures, collecting past-due accounts, and customer service, including lifetime value and customer grading. If properly examined, the contents of this chapter can have a major effect on higher profits.

Establishing Credit Policies and Procedures

Allowing customers and clients to defer payment for goods and services is a common and often necessary practice. Credit control is essential to controlling cash flow. Many companies go out of business because of management failure to distinguish between profits and cash flow. Credit control is comprised of policies, procedures, and practices that guarantee that the total amount of credit extended and the period for which it is extended are consistent with company policies.

Credit control prevents bad debts, controls cash flow, and increases profits. However, overly restrictive controls can sour relationships with good customers and slow company growth.

The following are suggested policies and procedures to be used in running your business:

1. Consider advanced payments, partial payments, or cash on delivery (COD).
2. Develop written credit policies that include
   a. sales terms
   b. sources to obtain credit information
   c. order approval
   d. reevaluation of credit to existing customers
   e. collection of past-due accounts
   f. authorization of settlements and write-offs
3. Place standard credit terms clearly on all invoices.
4. Obtain credit applications from all new customers.
5. Contact at least three supplier references from new customers.
6. Contact credit applicants' bank references.
7. Determine how many years the customer has been in business.
8. Determine the customer's payment experience with the supplier.
9. Assign credit limits to help contract limits.
10. Put all past-due accounts on Cash on Delivery (COD).
11. Check customers' credit limits and status of past-due accounts before orders are filled or services rendered.
12. Review credit limits for major customers at least annually.
13. Request personal guarantees for marginal credit applicants or past-due accounts.

14. Implement a quick and efficient mailing of invoices after goods are shipped or services rendered.
15. Send out monthly statements quickly and efficiently.

Collecting Past-Due Accounts

The following are seven key steps to collect past-due accounts.

1. Rely on phone calls as the primary collection technique. Use monthly statements, letters, and personal visits to supplement phone efforts.
2. Contact customers within a few days of the date an account becomes past due.
3. Document key information obtained during phone calls for future reference and follow-up.
4. Have the owner of the company get involved and contact the company when accounts become old.
5. Make sure the owner of the customer's company is contacted before a final demand letter is sent out.
6. Send final demand letters via certified mail.
7. Only the owner should authorize settlements or write-offs of accounts.

Customer Service

Being close to your customers allows you to respond to their demands, quickly act on facts instead of hunches, develop products or services better tailored to their needs, improve sales, and increase profits.

Successful customer service means making customers want to come back for more and getting them to refer you to others. Unless top management is committed to the concept of customer service, there is little chance that a customer service program will work. Everyone in an organization is responsible for customer service, even if their jobs do not involve direct customer contact.

Customer lifetime value is a way of measuring how much your customer is worth over the time they are your customers. Increasing customer retention can significantly increase sales and profits. New customer acquisitions should never be neglected, because existing business may decline for reasons outside of your control.

Here is a chart that shows how customer acquisition is monetized.

FIGURE 25.1 NEW VS. EXISTING CUSTOMER COSTS

	Attract New $20,000 Customer	Return of Existing $20,000 Customer
Time Investment	10 hours @ $150	4 hours @ $150
Opportunity Cost	$1,500	$600
Up-front Cost	$2,000	None
Profit Margin at 20%	$4,000	$4,000
Less Cost Above	$3,500	$600
Net Profit	$500	$3,400

CUSTOMER GRADING

Evaluating your customers and assigning them a grade will help you determine which customers you really want to spend your time, effort, and money on. You should, on an annual basis, grade your customers (A, B, C, and D). The following criteria may be used:

- Amount of revenue they bring in
- Number of goods or services they buy
- Percent of total sales revenue

- History of positive growth
- Profitability
- Collectability
- Willingness to give referrals
- Even flow of work
- No legal hazards
- Future purchasing needs

You should develop your own matrix of the above criteria based on what is important to your business. The higher-scoring customers are rated an "A." These customers should get the highest level of customer service. "D"-rated customers should be fired as soon as possible.

Customer management, credit collections, and customer service are three areas of a business that are not usually given the attention they deserve. As we have learned, customer management is one of the most important areas in managing a company for higher profits. Next, we'll look at marketing your business.

Chapter 26

Managing Marketing and Sales: Some Low-Cost Tips

By David J. Lucier, CPA

Let's start with a couple definitions. *Marketing* is everything you do to get in front of a potential customer, whether face-to-face, by phone, by a catalogue, by a website, or by e-mail. *Sales* are everything you do to close the customer. *Advertising* is included in marketing.

The following are no-cost or low-cost marketing and sales efforts often used by small businesses. You will probably never see most of these tips in business school. Business school case studies are always big businesses that have very expensive advertising budgets. An example of this would be a big business that can spend millions of dollars branding a new logo to potential customers. A small business can't do this. Therefore, a logo is not as important to a small business.

Let's start with the basics.

The Intangibles
Naming Your Business

The name you choose for your business might be one of the most important long-term marketing and branding decisions you make. The following are a number of factors to consider when choosing a name.

The business name must be easy to pronounce, easy to spell, and not misleading in any way. If possible, it is helpful if the name of the business also says what you do. Examples of this are Jiffy Lube®, Lucier CPA, Inc., and BMW of Newport.

Sometimes it is better to use a person's first or last name when naming a business. Customers often remember Ray the Carpenter, instead of Supreme Construction, if it is a small business.

What you do can also be explained in a tagline. An example of this is Walmart® discount store's "Save money. Live better" or Lucier CPA, Inc.'s "We Guarantee Success."

The name must be carefully selected to ensure copyright and trademark protection and incorporating in the states you will do business in both now and in the future. With many businesses today, the website name and e-mail address can be the most important part of a name selection. An example of this is amazon.com or pilatesjen.com. You should also explore search engine optimization (SEO) ahead of time.

Consideration should also be given to your telephone number. A great example of this is 1-800-FLOWERS.

As you can see from the above, the selection of the best name can be both a time-consuming and costly process. However, the right selection benefits the company for a lifetime.

Niches

A niche will differentiate your company from the competition. You should always be able to communicate both in writing and verbally five reasons you are better than the competition. High quality is one of the five that I have seen with most successful small businesses.

Testimonials

Testimonials are inexpensive, give great confidence and display credibility to a new customer. For these reasons they are extremely effective. They can be used in mailers, framed in the office, used as part of a presentation binder, posted on your website, advertised, or printed in brochures. You must ask customers to write them for you, and be prepared to assist the customer in the writing process.

Branding

Brand awareness would be remembering the name VOLVO. Brand-benefit awareness would be remembering that the name VOLVO means safety. Branding is more important now because of the increasing number of small businesses. Proper branding keeps the company top of mind with prospects and increases confidence and credibility. Branding must be consistently and repeatedly marketed in ads, brochures, signage, letters, business cards, newsletters, graphics, offices, and by word of mouth from salespeople and employees.

Tagline

A tagline is a set of words that describes the spirit of your company, your brand, your benefits, or your uniqueness. The VOLVO tagline is "For Life," for twenty years NIKE's was "Just Do It," and Allstate® uses "You're In Good Hands." The tagline must be short and believable. It should be winning, lasting, and memorable. The longer you use it, the more powerful it becomes. It should be used everywhere, including signage, ads, brochures, business cards, letters, and trade shows.

Geographic Marketing and Advertising

In his book *The 10-Minute Marketer's Secret Formulas: A Shortcut to Extraordinary Profits Using Neighborhood Marketing*, Tom Feltenstein writes that the majority of customers come from ten minutes or ten miles away from your business location.[ix] That means they either live or work ten minutes or ten miles away or are driving by your business. Some businesses in rural areas may need to increase this number to fifteen, twenty, or thirty, but the concepts are the same.

Based on the above, you should focus your advertising and marketing dollars on this group. This rules out most TV, radio, and major newspaper advertising, which usually reaches a much bigger market. There are many opportunities to market directly to your neighborhood. Here are eight:

1. Offer your product or service to local charities.
2. Sponsor various local sports or music teams.
3. Advertise on local bulletin boards.
4. Increase your signage.
5. Sponsor events like 10K races and give T-shirts.
6. Increase the use of advertising specialties.
7. Promote other local businesses that promote you.
8. Develop discount programs for local schools and charities.

Referral-Based Marketing System

Most successful small businesses have one thing in common. Most of their new customers come from referrals. In addition, they receive more referrals than they need. Therefore, they are able to:

1. Pick and chose the best new customers that fit their requirements, profit margins, consistency of buying patterns, etc.
2. Work their existing customer base to keep the profits high and service current needs
3. Predict staffing needs to maximize service efficiency (labor) and overhead utilization.

In *The Referral of a Lifetime: The Networking System that Produces Bottom-Line Results... Every Day! (The Ken Blanchard Series)*, by Tim Templeton and Lynda Rutledge Stephenson, the authors write about a survey that was performed for real estate agents. Eighty-five percent of their recent customers agreed that they would use this agent again if the need arose. However, three years later, of the 85 percent who used an agent again, only 10 percent used that original agent. When asked why they didn't use the original agent, they all said they forgot the agent or the agent didn't keep in touch with them.[x]

Consider this, if you know at least 250 people, and those 250 people each know an additional 250 people that is a total of 62,500 people. If you can develop strong relationships with your 250 people and get them to refer you to their 250 people, you potentially have access to 62,500 people. Think of your 250 people as your field salespeople.

Based on the above, staying in touch with past customers and friends is the best way of increasing referrals. The three best ways to accomplish this is by:

1. Mailings, newsletters, brochures, new product or service information, etc.
2. Birthday or holiday cards. (Note: Thanksgiving cards can be better than Christmas cards. Christmas cards should be mailed December 1, to be the first to arrive so that you stand out.)
3. Broadcast e-mail of newsletters, tips, or other information.

Dan Sullivan, founder of The Strategic Coach® Program, advises his workshop participants on The Referability Habits™:[iii]

1. To show up on time
2. Do what they say they are going to do
3. Finish what they start
4. Say please and thank you

The Tangibles

Business Cards

Your business card must be a mini brochure. Business cards are seen by more people than other forms of advertising. The card should list the following:

- Your name
- Business name
- Business address (with zip code)
- Phone number (with area code)
- Fax number
- E-mail address
- Web address
- Logo
- Company colors

The following are additional marketing items to consider for a business card:

- Specialization
- Awards
- Picture
- Services offered
- Benefits
- Tagline
- Testimonies
- Years in business
- Other

The card can be expanded to a fold-over card to increase available space. Many small-business owners claim that their business card is the most important marketing tool they have. Always smile when you pass one out, and include a card with all your mailings. This gently tells the recipient that you want referrals.

Signage, Outside

An outside sign can give you the best return on your marketing investment. It should be very clear to read from a distance with contrasting colors (for example, dark letters with a light background). Also, it is best to limit the number of words to six, since this is the maximum comfortably taken in at a single glance. Small A-signs on the street are great for additional signage. Taglines after your name are great for telling customers what you do and why you are different, and they reinforce your brand.

Signage, Inside

A high percentage of all purchases are made by inside signs. Retailers can use signage to merchandise products. Signs are like silent salespeople. Make sure your signs match your identity. You can use signs to differentiate your company from others—for example, "Highest Quality," "25 Years in Business," "Honesty," "Integrity," and "Raving Fan Service." You can also display framed magazine ads, newspaper articles, awards, degrees, and customer testimonial letters.

Newsletters

I and many of my clients have used newsletters for many years with great success. They are a great way to keep in constant contact with prospects and referral sources. I recommend one to four pages per issue four to six times per year. The articles should be short, easy to read, and give great value to the reader. They are also a great place to showcase your expertise on various subjects. Always encourage readers to contact you if they would like further information. Always include a business card (which subtly tells the reader you want referrals) or a referral postcard.

Customer Mailing List

To many companies, a customer mailing list can be the most valuable asset to the business. Without a list, most mail-order companies would go out of business. It is best to get this information at the point of sale. Stay in touch with customers on a regular basis regarding the following:

- Newsletter
- Asking for referrals
- Birthdays
- Specials
- Events
- Holidays

CUSTOMER CONTACT

Marketing doesn't end when the sale is made. You must stay in touch with your customers because if you don't, someone else will. Many companies lose money when the first sale is made. The big profit is with repeat sales. You should always send a thank-you card after the first sale is made. Eighty percent of business is lost because of apathy after the initial sale.

The following are proven ways to keep in touch:

- Newsletters
- Birthday cards
- Thank-you cards
- Holiday cards
- Telephone calls
- Lunches
- Ball games/events
- Advertising specialties
- Private sales
- Holiday parties

A CONSTANT FLOW OF NEW BUSINESS

Super-successful companies usually have more business than they can handle. Some turn away more than half of all new customers. This gives them the opportunity to pick only the ones that give them the best results. The best result is not only a high profit margin, but customers who pay their bills fast, refer their friends, and fit the organization's definition of a great customer.

Great companies always focus on keeping their existing customer base happy first, before chasing new ones.

Customer service is usually outstanding with these companies. They usually strive for raving fans customer service versus satisfied customers. The difference is that a raving fan customer will allow you to have higher margins, pay you faster, and refer more people. In short, they are very loyal to you.

Many of these companies use inexpensive marketing methods to increase referrals. The following are some of the more common ones these companies use:

1. Newsletters, usually four to six times per year.
2. Asking for referrals constantly.
3. Handing out business cards daily.
4. Returning phone calls promptly.
5. Thanking the referral source each time one is made.
6. Delivering consistent customer service.
7. Taking new referral sources to lunch two to four times per week.
8. Getting involved in exposure organizations (for example, chamber of commerce).
9. Attending Sandler Training.
10. Attending Dale Carnegie programs.
11. Developing basic social skills to get people to like you.
12. Being able, available, affordable, and affable.

Selling

Marketing is defined as anything you do to get in front of a customer. Selling is what you do to get the order (close the sale) when you are in front of the customer (face-to-face, on the phone, or through a website).

There are very few business courses in college or in MBA programs that address selling skills. Sandler Training is by far the best program, which uses a franchise-based system, offered in many parts of the country.

Clearly, lack of selling skills and lack of marketing skills are the two reasons businesses fail. It is amazing how business owners spend hours studying their craft and how little time they spend studying sales, marketing, or even finance.

One top business book author wrote that an individual has no business being in business unless he or she knows how to sell.

Small-business owners must always be selling. Owners should always be telling everyone they meet about their business. It is proper for a business owner to give everyone his business card.

Whether your customers come to your premises or not, you must constantly be hunting for leads, referrals, introductions, and appointments. You must constantly be calling on new customers, meeting new people, and cultivating new relationships.

Having a customer, getting a customer, and keeping a customer are more important than the product or service, management, finance, or anything else.

As you can see, there are many no-cost or low-cost marketing and sales tactics that can be used by small businesses. Figure out which ones work best for you, and include them in your marketing plan, as outlined in Chapter 7. And, if you're successful with your marketing techniques, you'll be expanding (the topic of our next chapter).

The following marketing and sales books are written with consideration for small business with limited budgets:

MARKETING

1. *The Referral of a Lifetime: The Networking System that Produces Bottom-Line Results… Every Day! (The Ken Blanchard Series)*, by Tim Templeton and Lynda Rutledge Stephenson

2. *Guerrilla Marketing: Easy and Inexpensive Strategies for Making Big Profits from Your Small Business,* 4th Ed. Jay Conrad Levinson with Jeannie Levinson and Amy Levinson
3. *Guerrilla Marketing for Free: Dozens of No-Cost Tactics to Promote Your Business and Energize Your Profits* by Jay Conrad Levinson
4. *Raving Fans: A Revolutionary Approach to Customer Service* by Ken Blanchard and Sheldon Bowles
5. *Book Yourself Solid: The Fastest, Easiest, and Most Reliable System for Getting More Clients Than You Can Handle Even if You Hate Marketing and Selling.* by Michael Port
6. *Purple Cow: Transform Your Business by Being Remarkable.* by Seth Godin

SALES
1. *Never Eat Alone: And Other Secrets to Success, One Relationship at a Time* by Keith Ferrazzi and Tahl Raz
2. *You Can't Teach a Kid to Ride a Bike at a Seminar: The Sandler Sales Institute's 7-Step System for Successful Selling* by David H. Sandler and John Hayes
3. *Close the Deal: 120 Checklists for Sales Success* by Sam Deep and Lyle Sussman
4. *Mr. Shmooze: The Art and Science of Selling Through Relationships* by Richard Abraham
5. *How to Win Friends & Influence People* by Dale Carnegie

Chapter 27

Managing Growth and Expansion

By R. Sean Manning, CPA

It requires real dedication to move from a sales and marketing approach to one of business expansion. To expand, business owners might need to either hire someone to take on the role of expansion or move into the role themselves. If they decide to enter that role themselves, they will most likely need to step away from other duties and hire staff to assist in those areas.

When talking to most successful business owners, the word growth brings feelings of joy and optimism. This is a result of knowing good growth can bring greater success and increased revenue. With growth comes new challenges and the need to meet customers' expectations. You may need to hire staff, invest in equipment and inventory, and continue to service your customers at their expectation levels. If you can successfully grow and meet the increased challenges associated with the growth, I would say you have successfully managed growth. Most businesses thrive on managed growth, so the challenge is to find a growth level that is manageable for your business. While managed growth can lead to success, unmanaged growth can lead to problems or bad growth.

When Can Growth Be Bad?

Growth is bad when the business products or services start to deteriorate due to rapid growth or growth that has created unmanageable challenges. This might result in the owner's inability to forecast and prepare for a new challenge. For example, a business that is in the service industry must be staffed for growth. That would require the business owner to anticipate the growth, start hiring and training staff to meet the new customer requests, and be prepared to manage the services being performed.

Staffing for growth requires time and money, so the challenge then becomes when to make the decision to hire and train before it is too late. If you are too late, you could miss the opportunity to service your new customers' needs. If you fall short of their expectations, there is a good possibility you will lose that customer. If you hire and train too soon, you could create cash flow problems and false expectations of staff that result in unsatisfied employees. Use all available tools to avoid circumstances of bad growth and understand the risks associated with it so that your business does not suffer as a result of bad growth.

Few businesses can open their doors and rely upon a group of customers for the life of their business. Most businesses require a steady stream of new and returning customers. Previously we talked about having a marketing plan. A growth plan is the execution and management of that marketing plan. Growth can be slow and managed or very fast. Each business is very different relating to growth. Some businesses have growth limits or restrictions that require additional decision making and planning.

Developing a Growth Plan

A growth plan delegates the marketing of the business. It could require creating a division that includes sales managers and salespeople. The following is a summary of areas to consider during growth:

Customer Service

If your business has a reputation for having great customer service, which should be a goal of every business, rapid growth could create obstacles that begin to deteriorate your quality of service. You must make a conscious effort to develop policies and systems that maintain the customer service that your customers come to expect.

Staff and Training

Growth most often creates a need for additional staff. Hiring and maintaining qualified staff can be a full-time job in itself. As your business grows, maintaining a plan on how your staff is hired and trained will be very important. Look for additional opportunities to develop the staff's skills and knowledge. The amount of resources available to a business owner in a global market is vast and should be monitored continually.

Technology

Technology is advancing more quickly every year. Technology can provide opportunity, but it can also create problems. If technology advancement in your industry is not monitored and adapted when necessary, you can face an uncertain future. A growth plan could cause delays in investing in and implementing new technology, sometimes the very technology that allows a business to grow more efficiently. We recommend you always monitor the technology that allows your business to thrive.

Capital Investment

Growth requires capital investment. Investment in staff, equipment, and facilities are just a few of the most obvious examples. When you blend your marketing plan with the growth plan and the budget, you could determine that more rapid growth might not be the preferred path for the long-term success of your business and therefore avoid the additional capital investment.

Monitor the Competition

Finally, consider a plan to continue to monitor the competition that will allow you to maintain a competitive edge in your business market. This will not only require you to manage your growth but also study the competition. By studying the competition you can find ways to better market your business and adapt more quickly to changes in your industry and the opportunities they present.

Rapid Growth

What is rapid growth, and who is best suited for this? Rapid growth is defined as a growth rate of at least 20 percent. Therefore, if sales were $1 million last year, this year sales would need to be *more* than $1.2 million to be considered a rapidly growing business. This is best suited for businesses that have prepared for the growth and have put resources in place to make the growth successful. Business can experience expansive growth through acquisition or implementation of an aggressive marketing or sales campaign. Both examples require a well-thought-out strategy and are not necessarily right for all businesses and/or business owners.

Keep an open mind when it comes to growth—not only for the opportunity but also for the risks and challenges that come with growth. Monitor your business plan, budget, and financials so that you are prepared for growth opportunities and can evaluate their validity and make the proper decision regarding implementation.

Once you've expanded and grown your business, it might be time to think about moving on to the fifth step of this book: building a saleable business.

Step 5:

Building a Salable Business and the Sale

CHAPTER 28

IS IT TIME TO SELL?

By R. Sean Manning, CPA

"The number one reason small business owners want to sell is stress and the number one cause of stress to the small business owner is employees."
—Jeff Guinn,
LGI Business Brokers, Columbia, Missouri

Planning for and properly positioning your business to be sold can be one of the most rewarding aspects of owning your own business. Likewise, failing to plan for the sale or transition of your business can leave a business owner unfulfilled and disappointed with the sale or, in some cases, closure without a sale.

There are often one of two reasons that someone starts a new business. The first is that an unexpected opportunity or a circumstance arises which results in a new business. Because these types of businesses are created almost overnight, there is obviously not much planning involved. Some examples include the following: a salesman given a unique or exclusive product to sell that requires that he start a business to market and sell the product; a professional suddenly laid off and then given a short-term solution by working for himself, which later becomes permanent; or even a roll of the dice by one or more people who just think they have a better way to do something. These examples might require someone to quickly form a business, often resulting in quick success and eventually the question of what's next. These people are less likely to have a business plan. They are often very self-motivated and good decision makers. Because of their quick success, the planning process might be slow to mature, leaving possible opportunity failures in the future. This type of business owner must dedicate himself to start a plan and look into the future for new opportunities.

The second reason someone starts a new business is more calculated and planned. In this situation, the business owner plans out in detail when the business will start, how it will run, and what success might look like. Although this type of owner is very organized, the possible opportunity loss he might experience is when a quick response is needed. He might let the opportunity go, just because he doesn't have enough information to make a 100 percent complete and accurate decision. These types of people often own independent or franchise businesses that require more critical analysis and usually more financial capital to get off the ground.

It is important to note when it comes to selling or transitioning your business that proper planning and personal expectations should be considered in preparation for the event. You might want to consider how you started your business. When it comes to selling your business, it is best to have a plan, and those who have worked with a plan in the past are usually better prepared to transition their business when the time comes.

Remember, it is never too soon or too late to start preparing for the transition of your business. Many business owners we have interviewed would like to sell, and are planning on selling their business to their children or close family members. The reality is that only a small percentage of all businesses are sold to children or close family members. It is very important to keep an open mind when it comes to your business and who the best buyer is. Although most businesses are sold based upon the financial condition of the business, sometimes a strategic buyer targets the business for acquisition, and that can result in a very rewarding sale for the seller.

Complete a Self-Evaluation

First assess if you are personally ready to sell. A lot of emotions come into play, not only in planning to sell a business but also when a business is sold. There are many people who simply should not sell their business. If they did, they would become depressed. The depression occurs due to a number of things, but most often because they have either lost their livelihood or sold something that is truly a part of them. Other people feel rewarded and completely satisfied when they sell their business. These people have separated themselves from the business and look at the business more as an investment.

How will you feel when you sell your business? Just by asking yourself this simple question, you will start to prepare yourself for the feelings you will go through if you decide to sell your business. It is very important to understand how you will feel.

Evaluate your liabilities and personal obligations. Both in the business and at a personal level, business owners might enter into a number of financial obligations. These financial obligations exist for many reasons, but most often they are from lending sources. When a business is sold, there could be a number of financial obligations created either prior to the sale or as a result of the sale. It will be important to assess the various obligations and the resulting amount that needs to be met during or after the sale. This assessment will help determine if the owner is in a financial position to sell from a financial obligation standpoint.

To get a better understanding of financial obligations that you might not be thinking about, consult with your trusted advisers.

They should help you study the possible results of the sell and uncover hidden costs, like future tax liabilities, legal obligations, or even future financial commitments based on your future financial plan.

Complete a long-term financial plan. The financial plan generally looks at current assets and any assets created from the sale of the business. These assets are then compared to a number of other factors, like inflation, lifestyle, age, and return on investment to determine if the assets will be sufficient for the business owner to retire comfortably as a result of the sale. Often this gives an owner a baseline of what is needed if a business is sold. The business then can be professionally reviewed and even appraised to determine if the proceeds from the sale can meet the financial goals of the owner. If they do, the next option might be to sell the business. If not, the business owner should develop a plan that will meet his needs sometime in the future.

Variables, like age, marital status, number of children and their age, charity goals, and personal spending habits, can all have a dramatic influence on someone's financial future, so a plan that is right for one person could be far from adequate for another person. An adequate plan will uncover many financial obligations that may have been overlooked.

The buyer's perceived value is what determines the market value of the business and not only what someone is willing to pay, but also how you get paid. We can all wish for the stars and dream of big dollars, but if the seller's perceived value is not the same as the buyer's, you will have a difficult time not only finding a buyer but also having negotiations that result in a successful transaction.

If you think you want to sell your business, remember, it is never too early to start planning. Try to develop a business that can operate without you, and continue to prepare yourself mentally and financially for the sale of your business. Next, we'll discuss valuation of a business so that you can become more familiar with the income potential from the sale of your business.

Chapter 29

Selling and Valuing Your Business

By R. Sean Manning, CPA

"Over 60% of all businesses have less than $500,000 in sales and less than 5 employees. These will generally be less profitable and bring a lower sales price because they don't have systems in place to run without an owner." [x]

—Tier2Brokers.com

Earlier in the business operations chapters, we discussed working on your business and not in your business. Now we are going to take that to the next level. When it comes to selling a business, the business that is worth the most money is the one that runs without any involvement from the owner. We have talked a lot about this concept throughout the book so let us go into more detail now as to why that is so important.

There are many reasons people decide to sell a business, but before you decide to sell, take a minute to look at the underlying reason for the sale and how it will affect your life and the lives of others. Sometimes the owner is just stressed, tired, or bored. If that is the case, it might make more sense to step back and hire a CEO to run your business than to sell. Oftentimes this new CEO will bring in fresh ideas to grow the business. The end result is that the owner makes more money and increases the value of the business while getting relief from the stress or boredom.

There are other times when a sale makes more sense. If the owner is unable to handle the business due to age, and the family members have no interest, then it is time to sell. Another example would be if trends are changing and the whole industry is in a decline. In a declining industry there is often a buyer who needs your business to complement theirs, and you can still realize a fair value in the sale.

If you do decide to sell, you should also consider family members and loyal longtime employees. You can't protect your employees forever, but you can try to negotiate some job protections as part of the sale or use part of the sale proceeds to reward those who helped you build the business. Then there are the family members. Some might have a sentimental attachment to the business, and some might just see dollar signs in the form of an inheritance. For those who truly are a part of the business, it makes sense to get their input about the sale process. For others, it is sad to say that money can often create greed and jealousy. There is probably little you can do to avoid those issues, so always maintain your integrity and fairness, and make sure you have a strong estate plan to protect what you worked so hard to achieve.

WHAT IS THE VALUE?

Most people would not pay a fee for the privilege of going to work somewhere. However, most small-business owners often think the value of their business is whatever they show as profit. The real value of the business is more likely based on what the profit is after the business pays a fair salary for the services provided by the owner. In many cases the profits are less than the salary would be to hire someone for the ownership duties, and basically the business has no value. That is the first concept the business owner must grasp.

In the big publicly traded corporations, stockholders elect a board of directors, who give guidance to the president, who manages the day-to-day operations. If someone wants to buy a business and just make profits from the business the same as he would share in the profits of Walmart® by owning company stock, then the duties must be separated. As the president/manager of the company, you make day-to-day decisions and run the operations. As a stockholder or equity holder, you are entitled to your share of the profits after all salaries are paid. If you buy the business, you need to know whether the president/manager will stay on to run the company. Most small-business owners sell their company because they are tired of the management issues. If you buy a company and the management changes, everyone knows there is a greater risk you will lose customers, good employees, and the like. Therefore, buying a company without the management will always result in a lower purchase price to factor in the unknown.

If you look at the statistic from Tier2Brokers.com above, you will note that over 60 percent of all businesses have less than five employees and less than $500,000 in sales. These businesses generally have not been able to separate the management and compensation issues from ownership and will be more difficult to sell. The key for the business owner is to constantly work toward putting key people in place so that the business will run without the owner being present. This could mean fewer profits today, but the trade-off is a more valuable business and free time for the owner. Ask yourself which model will help you achieve your dreams.

Now that we separated the value of a job from the business value, it is time to value the business.

What Is the Business Worth?

A business that runs without the owner involved is generally a more valuable business than one that requires the owner be present to be successful.

When it comes to determining value of a business, we start with some basic formulas. These formulas are meant to be a starting point for determining value, and it is very important to understand that there are other important aspects of valuing a business. Some of the important aspects include staffing, organization, location, uniqueness, and customer/client loyalty. Additionally, the buyer ultimately decides if what he is buying is worth the investment. To start, let's take a look at a typical small business.

FIGURE 29.1 TYPICAL SMALL BUSINESS FINANCIAL

	Typical Small Business Financial	
	Sales	2,000,000.00
	Direct Costs	500,000.00
Total Assets = $650,000.00	Gross Profit	$1,500,000.00
	Overhead Costs	750,000.00
	Interest	25,000.00
	Depreciation	50,000.00
	Amortization	25,000.00
	Owner Wages	75,000.00
	Net Profit (before taxes)	$575,000.00

VALUATION FORMULA ONE

The first basic formula is to look at gross sales and take a multiple of gross sales. Multiples can range from .5 to 1.5 or higher depending on the type of business. This valuation technique is used more in the service industry. If we assume our business normally lists for 1.1 times the annual gross sales, this business would list for $2,200,000.00 (2,000,000.00 * 1.1).

VALUATION FORMULA TWO

The second basic formula is to look at net profit and use a multiple that typically ranges from 3 to 5 times net profit. If you use the low end of 3 times, the business would be worth $1,725,000.00 (575,000.00 * 3) and the high end would be worth $2,875,000.00 (575,000.00 * 5). Sometimes rather than use net profit, the valuation will be on a modification of net profit using the businesses earnings before interest, depreciation and amortization (EBIDA). Using EBIDA in the formula has the effect of determining value based more on cash flow than on net income.

VALUATION FORMULA THREE
A third basic formula is to take a percentage of business assets. For example, 2 times assets would be $1,300,000.00 (650,000.00 * 2).

All of the previous formulas give us a general starting point. There are also a number of other items to consider, which I will list and describe briefly.

Assets: Typically assets are added to formulas one and two. Formula three only considers assets for the basis of the valuation.

EBIDA (Earnings before Interest, Depreciation, and Amortization): Used in formula two to increase net income for valuation purposes: (575,000.00 + 25,000.00 + 50,000.00 + 25,000.00) = 675,000.00

Owner Wages: Owner wages and owner benefits may be considered in the valuation. An owner that is less involved with the day-to-day operations of the business may drive the price higher than an owner that is crucial to the business operations.

Intangible Assets: These are nonmonetary assets the business has created. The value of the business often includes intangible assets that may or may not be listed as assets on the company financial statements. Examples of these intangible assets might include copyrights, trademarks, goodwill, customer lists, and noncompete agreements.

We have just touched on the basics of valuing a business. It becomes very evident if you are ever involved with the purchase or sale of a business that there are vast arrays of additional considerations. These include staffing skills, organizational structure, the efficiencies of the business, its location, and the customer/client perception. It is vital to start planning your business sale years in advance to become familiar with the process and the possible valuation of the business. In my experience, business owners tend to value their business higher than the market will bear. If you and your advisers are having a difficult time determining the value of the business, you might want to consider having a formal valuation done.

Never lose sight that you have an opportunity to build value in your business every day. If you adopt this thought process, the road to success in the sale of your business will be greatly improved. Also be sure to plan personally for the sale so that you are satisfied with your lifestyle after the sale.

The sale of any business has tax consequences; our next chapter offers advice on this important topic.

CHAPTER 30

Tax Planning for the Sale

By C. Gregory Orcutt, CPA

The sale of your business might be years away; however, it is never too early to consider the tax consequences. There are things you can do now to minimize the tax you will pay. For many business owners, their business is their largest asset. Early planning could save thousands of dollars in taxes. Do not wait until you are ready to sell before reviewing the tax issues; do it now.

Assets and Equity

Businesses are usually sold by the owners selling the stock-equity they have or by selling the assets. Most business buyers will want to buy your assets and not your stock-equity. It is to the buyer's advantage to buy your assets so they do not also buy your past or future liabilities and they are able to depreciate or amortize the assets they buy. You will have a very simple tax transaction if you sell your stock-equity but be sure to discuss the details with your accountant. Since most small businesses sold are asset sales, that is the type of sale we will focus on and discuss in more detail.

A business has many different types of assets, such as equipment, furniture and fixtures, real estate, accounts receivable, and intangible assets. When the assets are sold, the gain or loss is calculated on each asset. The basis of the asset is the purchase price less any depreciation taken. The tax rate applied to the gain will depend upon the length of time owned and how much depreciation has been taken. The best tax rates are for long-term capital gains, and the worst rate is for ordinary income. Usually an asset sale has both capital gains and ordinary income, so the more profit that is capital gain, the better.

The type of entity that sells the assets will determine who will pay the tax. The worst entity to sell the assets from is a C corporation, because there will be two levels of tax paid. One tax is assessed at the corporate level and the second at the shareholder level. The corporate-level tax will be at the normal tax rates that could be as high as 35 percent, and then depending upon how the sale proceeds are paid to the shareholders, they could pay tax of 15 to 35 percent on what is received. This is why early planning for the sale of a business is important. If your business is a C corporation, you need to determine whether a conversion to an S corporation is possible.

If the assets are sold from a sole proprietorship, partnership, or S corporation, then the tax will be paid by the owners. Some of the tax will be at capital gains rates, and the balance will be at ordinary rates.

Installment Sale

Often a business is sold and the seller provides the financing for the buyer. This is called an installment sale. The tax is paid as the cash is received by the seller. A ratio is calculated at the time of the sale so that future cash payments can be allocated between a return of capital and profit. That ratio is applied to the principal of the loan payments received each year to determine how much is taxable.

Stock Exchange

If a business is selling to a larger company, they may offer to exchange stock rather than pay cash. A stock exchange can be a good tax strategy, because tax is only paid on the cash received. When the seller sells the stock they received in the exchange, tax will be paid. If the stock received is not sold for many years, the tax will be deferred, which allows the proceeds to continue to grow. There is a big risk that the stock the buyer is receiving loses value or underperforms compared to what the money could have returned. Your advisers will have to take all of these issues into account before you accept an exchange of stock.

The taxes on the sale of your business will be the largest expense. A well-thought-out plan can help reduce the tax or possibly defer the tax to future years. Oftentimes the structure of the sale will cost one party more tax but save tax for the other. Make sure you are getting professional advice early in the negotiations so that you understand the tax consequences.

Chapter 31

Who Are the Buyers?

By Bert Doerhoff, CPA

In the last chapter, we talked about tax planning for the sale. Now is the time to talk about who wants to buy a business and why. Every business owner will dispose of their business at some time, so no business book would be complete without a discussion of buyers. Even if you die with your business, someone will have to pass it on to the next owner, so you need to understand what that owner is looking for. If that new owner happens to be your children, wouldn't you want them to have the best possible chance of success in continuing your business?

What Buyers Want

Buyers are often looking for factors that will make buying and taking over a new business easy. These are as follows:

A Business That Runs without the Owner
Every buyer wants a business that will pay for itself over a reasonable period of time after paying fair wages and all expenses.

One of the big questions in the buyer's mind relating to how the business will pay for itself is how the business will perform in the future without the old owner in the picture. Most business owners want to be involved in every decision and don't think about how that decreases the value of their business. If you train others how to make key decisions in your business so it runs without you, then there is less uncertainty for the potential buyer. This may be a real blow to your ego to think employees can do as good a job as you, the owner. In some cases, you will be right and your decision will be better, but in others you will see improvements on your ideas. The sooner you start this process, the sooner you increase the marketability of your business, because there are more potential buyers.

There is a whole list of angel investors and venture capital people out there with money to spend, but they have no time or interest in running another business. They want a business with great growth potential and a great management team in place who can run the operation without assistance.

A Business with Niche Product or Large Market Share

The next step is to look at your market size and market share. Buyers within your industry are looking at how they can gain a competitive advantage. They already know your industry, but there is a substantial value to having the biggest market share. When you have market share, you also automatically have credibility. That means when the biggest businesses are looking for your product or service, you can generally get a premium price because you don't have to prove you can deliver, whereas smaller competitors have to overcome that hurdle. Therefore, controlling a unique market niche or a large share of your market adds your largest competitors as potential buyers at a premium price.

You might think all this talk about market share only applies to a bigger business than you could ever achieve. As the author of this chapter, I looked at my personal client base of small-business clients for an example. I have a client who started a wholesale business from scratch several years ago. He has recently received offers from competitors in the industry that are almost double what other businesses in that industry are selling for today. This premium offer is more than any individual would pay for the business simply because the competitor wants access to what my client has achieved. You too can command a premium value for your business if you can make what you have unique.

A Business with a Cause, Such as Environmental

In this day and age, being environmentally friendly is extremely popular. Anything with the green designation seems to help industry look good to the world, and many nations are putting incentives on the use of green products. Therefore, you need to look at your product or service and see how it can be tailored to respond to the environmental concerns of some industries. You might never have thought of your business this way, but if you can in some way support a cause that is important to an industry, you will have a new list of competitive buyers. I recently took part in some business negotiations between an international corporation and a start-up waste-to-energy business. The international corporation was looking for a way to be the first in the industry to not only sell their product but also to take care of disposal when it is used up and recycle the used product back into new products. Green is a much bigger cause today than at any time in the past, so do not ignore *green*.

A Business That Is Affordable in Terms of Financing

Many people have the dream of owning their own business. Most of them expect the bank to loan them 100 percent of the purchase price, because the buyers are certain they can succeed in the business. Unfortunately, banks don't want to be owners of a business; they want to lend money and get it repaid. That means if you are the buyer, you must have a good down payment to cover the equity. Most people starting out in business today have very little equity so they look for creative ways to come up with equity. One of those ways is to ask the seller to finance a portion of the sale. The bank will always want the first lien on the business, and that will mean the seller will have to take a second lien behind the bank. That also means that if the buyer does not succeed in the business, the seller has to pay off the bank loan and take the business back, or the seller just abandons the loan they financed and loses that part of the sale price. If a seller is willing to take some risk and finance, there are many more potential buyers, but the seller will want to negotiate protections in the contract to ensure that the business succeeds.

Potential Buyers

Sell to the Employees

If the owner has structured the business so it will truly run without the owner and has a good management team in place, some of the best potential buyers are the employees themselves. There are special tax incentives to the owners and the employees if they buy the business using a formal plan called an employee stock ownership plan (ESOP). If you think about it, who would know your business better and have the best chance of success? Normally that would be your key employee group. With an ESOP, the company is valued and the ESOP borrows the money to buy the company. Then the profits of the company are used to pay back the loan and eventually the employees own the company.

Pass the Business on to Your Family

If you have children, parents, or siblings who work in the business and have risen to the level of management, they are a great market for your business. The decision you have to make is whether to sell to them now and let them pay for the business or let them inherit the business when you die. They will want to buy so that they can control their destination, but you as an owner might like the profits and don't want to pay the big tax on the sale price. This can be a touchy negotiation, particularly if there are family members who are not a part of the business. The best advice is to determine the method of calculating the sale price immediately and sign agreements that legally bind all parties so that there are no questions later. It is always better to bring an independent third party in on these negotiations to try and keep things fair for all involved.

Look to Your Trade Association for a List of Competitors

If you are looking for a potential list of buyers, your competitors are always one of those potentials, and your trade association is a good place to get that list. However, be careful when offering a business for sale to a competitor. If the negotiations fail, there is always the chance your customers will find out your business is for sale and start to leave. Therefore, always find out all you can about your competition, including their morals and ethics, before you start any negotiations.

Buyout Events

If you have a partner or other owners in the business, there may be key events that can trigger a buy/sell agreement, such as death, disability, loss of a professional license, bankruptcy, commission of a felony, and more. These items should have all been clearly defined when forming the business, and the method of calculating the sale price should be a part of those items. Even though this might not be the buyer you had envisioned when you started the business, it is a very real potential, and determining what events trigger a buyout and the sale price should be done when shareholders think there is no possibility they could happen. If you wait until some sort of event happens that leads some owners to pressure others, things will most certainly end up in court. Past experience has shown the only parties happy when the litigation is over are the attorneys. Therefore, heed this warning: *If you have other owners in your business, put a buy/sell agreement in place while the honeymoon is still on.*

OTHER SOURCES OF BUYERS

There are many other potential places to look for buyers, including business brokers and advertising in major markets for someone moving into your area, to name two. Just be aware that in any business negotiation the value of your years of service and all your hard work will only be valued in terms of cash flow, the value of your assets, or the value of your market. The ego value of all your years of building the business is not important to the buyer, so before you look to sell, take that out of the equation and have your advisers tell you a fair value from the buyer's perspective so that you start with a reasonable number. There is nothing wrong with asking a premium price because you can always come down. However, make sure you can justify that price as being reasonable in some way.

In summary, there are lots of places to look for buyers once you spend the time building a salable business. Just make sure you take the time to work with that buyer to make sure you have found the right fit for your business so it will continue to succeed. Once you find that potential buyer, it is time to start negotiating the terms of the sale.

Chapter 32

Negotiating the Sale

By Bert Doerhoff, CPA

"About 20% of all businesses are for sale at any one time—smaller businesses are less likely to sell—some have unrealistic expectations."[xi]
—Tier2Brokers.com

Once you have someone interested in buying your business, you will probably want to celebrate, but that is when the real negotiations start. Buyers want to buy at the lowest price and get assurances they can get part of the sale price back if anything goes wrong. Sellers, on the other hand, want the highest price, want it all in cash, and want to walk out the door. You spent all that time building a salable business, so now you need to know how to not give it all away as you negotiate the sale. Here are some steps to making the sale go more smoothly.

Confidentiality or Nondisclosure Agreements

The very first step in these negotiations is to protect your business in the event the sale never takes place. You should consider having an agreement which obligates the potential buyer, and anyone they use to assist them, to not disclose anything about your business or the potential sale to others. Additionally, you will want them to return all information relating to your business should the sale not go through. Without this protection, here is an example of what could happen:

A potential buyer can find out who your customers are and approach each one of them and say they may want to start looking at other businesses because your business is for sale. Rumors about a sale can make people wonder if you are failing. You simply cannot afford to risk the reputation and trust you worked so hard to build. Make it very clear from the start of any negotiations the importance you place on confidentiality and your intentions to follow through if there is any violation of confidentiality.

Negotiate the Big Picture with a Handshake First

The problem in business sale negotiations is that everyone is looking for what can go wrong. With that attitude, it is easy to lose sight of the big picture. There is a buyer who wants to buy and a seller who wants to sell. Don't let attorneys start drafting any documents until you and the potential buyer sit down over coffee with a pencil and a napkin and document the big terms of the sale and the benefits to both parties. After that, start negotiating all the little things, but always keep that big picture in front of you during the negotiations.

As CPAs, we have all seen many sales where the negatives and the cost of documents got out of hand. Keep in mind you had to do something right to get your business where it is today. The other parties might be telling you everything you did wrong, but remember they wouldn't even be talking if they saw no value in what you have. Make sure everyone in the negotiations understands value from the view of buyer and seller so it can be the common thread to come back to during the entire process. If you don't understand what others see as value, you can't phrase your negotiations to address that value.

Keep Negotiations Private from Staff and Customers

The negotiations should not take place at your place of business. If your customers and/or employees think you are selling out, it creates uncertainty in their mind. Customers and employees are the keys to success of your business, so if either feels you are abandoning them, they lose a part of their security blanket. You simply cannot afford to lose what you worked so hard to achieve. There will come a time and place to notify both customers and employees, and those topics are addressed in later chapters. The sale negotiation is not that time. Therefore, do your negotiations at a confidential, neutral site where there is little chance someone will see buyer and seller together and assume there is a potential sale.

The Buyer Generally Wants Your Assets, Not Your Entity

Legal and tax issues have a major impact on the structure of a final sale. Whoever owns your legal entity (sole proprietorship, LLC, S corporation, etc.) is responsible for whatever may have gone wrong in your business in the past, regardless of whether you are even aware you had a problem. Therefore, in most cases the buyer will want to buy your business name, goodwill, phone numbers, assets, et cetera, but will not want to buy your legal entity. In some cases, larger public corporations will buy the entire legal entity, but the majority of business sales do not include the sale of the legal entity. When a buyer does buy the entity, there will be a clause in the contract that requires you as the seller to reimburse them for any claims relating to when you owned the business. However, once you sell, you will have no control over, say, how much they spend defending those claims. That means your choice of entity is extremely important. In addition, with some entities you can have a big tax cost when you take the sale proceeds out of the legal entity that owned the business. The tax issues of a sale are discussed earlier in Chapter 30: "Tax Planning for the Sale."

CONSIDER AN EARN-OUT CLAUSE

An earn-out is an agreement where, if the business meets certain goals, the seller gets an increase in the selling price. Often the earn-out is the only way to truly get parties to agree on a selling price, because as the seller you think you are selling a great business with huge potential, but the buyer is asking how to pay for this business if it does not meet your projections. For example, the earn-out can increase the sale price if sales or profit goals are achieved. However, this can be a double-edged sword and the buyer may want it to work both ways. That means if things really fall apart after the sale, they will want to reduce the sale price. With all earn-outs the negotiations need to center around what is fair, reasonable, and achievable. The buyer will look at these as a great way to ensure you work hard to transition your employees and customers to stay with the business after the sale.

WHO SHOULD YOU HAVE ON THE SALE NEGOTIATION TEAM?

You built your business on your own and you will most likely think you can sell it on your own. Generally that is a mistake because you will sell one business in your life, and you need advisers who can see what might go wrong with the experience of consulting on many business sales. Look at it this way: if you cost yourself $20,000 by missing a tax or legal issue, undervaluing the business, or something else, you could have paid several top-quality advisers to work with you and save you that money. You are probably not surprised that we, as CPAs, suggest the first person you involve is the CPA. In addition, you need an attorney, and you might need to spend some time with business brokers, valuation specialists, and/or specialists in your industry to understand how others have valued similar businesses.

In summary; always start with the big picture, keep it confidential, make smart business decisions, be creative with ways to resolve differences, and always be fair and realistic. Those are some of the keys to negotiating a business sale. In the next chapter we move from the handshake agreement to putting it all on paper with the sale documents.

Chapter 33

Sale Documents and Escrows for Contingencies

By Bert Doerhoff, CPA

In the last chapter we cautioned against getting too excited when you find someone who wants your business until you get through negotiating the deal. Once you complete those negotiations, it is time to get down to drafting documents. Since you worked a lifetime to build this business, don't sign anything on the sale unless you understand the document. It is a good idea to have your trusted advisors review all the sales documents with you before you sign.

Here is a partial list of questions to answer regarding the sale:

Accounts receivable: Does buyer or seller get the balance owed by customers as of the date of the sale? Sometimes the buyer will ask the seller to guarantee collectability. An example of how that might work would be that the seller agrees that the buyer receives all accounts receivable as of the date of closing, and that sale price will be reduced by any accounts not collected within ninety days of the sale.

Other times the seller will keep the accounts receivable. Then the seller would need to determine who will collect those receivables. The buyer may agree to collect them and forward the money to the seller because the buyer does not want customers getting contacts for payments from two conflicting sources. The buyer and seller should decide how payments are applied as they come in. One solution could be that all payments will be applied first to receivables of seller for the first 90–120 days so it is clear the buyer is not just protecting his own interest. After this 90–120-day period, the buyer could turn the remaining accounts over to the seller to collect as he sees fit, so the buyer does not have to do old collections work on the seller's delinquent accounts. Buyer and seller should also negotiate what type of collections will be allowed on those accounts.

Accounts payable and bank loans: Buyer and seller will want to discuss who is responsible to pay the debts your business has at the date of sale and what happens if those are not paid. One suggestion would be that whichever party gets the collections from the receivables will also be responsible for paying the outstanding accounts payable as of the date of the sale. However, this can come back to haunt you, as the seller, if you are not careful. I have seen businesses run up their accounts payable as they grow their business. When the buyer comes in they may agree to pay those payables as part of the purchase. However, if the buyer starts to have cash flow problems and does not pay off those payables the vendors may try and ask the seller for repayment regardless of the fact the business has been sold. This is just another example of how, once you sell, you lose control, so make sure you understand the worst thing that can happen in the event of a sale.

Inventory: In most cases the inventory will sell as a part of the business. The seller often wants to get paid for the business and extra for the value of the inventory. However, the buyer will say he is buying the business based on the earnings it generates and it takes a set amount of inventory to generate those earnings. Therefore, that inventory is included as part of the sale price. Other issues that can come up in the sale negotiations deal with excess and obsolete inventory. The buyer will often want to reduce the sale price for obsolete inventory, which has been on hand longer than the industry standard. There are often industry ratios that show the average times per year inventory sells for a particular business. If the ratios show that a business normally carries inventory to cover six months' worth of sales, the seller may say he will reduce the sale price by any inventory on hand that is over nine months old. The other side of that negotiation is excess inventory. Many mature businesses carry much more inventory than their competitors because the owner has very low debt and generally has the opinion that you can't sell it if you don't own it. If the buyer is valuing the business based on industry standards, then the seller may want the ability to sell down the inventory to that standard or else receive additional compensation for the excess inventory he carries.

Working capital requirements: Oftentimes the buyer will ask the seller to have a minimum amount of working capital as of the date of the sale. The accounting definition of working capital is the difference between current assets and current liabilities. Current assets are things the business owns or are owed and include cash, accounts receivable, inventory, prepaid insurance, and anything else the business owns that will be used within a twelve-month period. Current liabilities are items the business owes and include accounts payable, payroll taxes payable, income taxes payable, principal due on loans within twelve months, et cetera. In simple terms, working capital is the difference between the assets (such as cash and receivables) that you will be able to use in the next twelve months and what you owe during the next twelve months (such as payroll taxes and accounts payable). It is the net of assets and liabilities that you have available to meet operating needs of the business on a day-to-day basis.

If the buyer expects to continue to operate the business, he doesn't want the seller, to quit paying bills to suppliers and pocket all the cash so the business can't meet obligations. Therefore, you may want to negotiate that the amount of working capital at the date of the sale will be no less than was on hand at the end of the last fiscal year or some other date not affected by the sale.

Lost customers: If your business has some major customers that would have a negative effect on business profits if you lost those customers, the buyer may want some guarantees on those customers. The buyer is paying for your business with the cash flow he obtains from the profits, so if the cash flow drops, he may want a reduction in the sale price. The amount of reduction could be negotiated based on the profit those customers generated for the business. This gives the seller incentive to do everything possible to transition the customers to stay with the business.

Guaranteed transaction level: Many industries have key operating statistics which a buyer will use when valuing a business. For example, the nursing home industry uses costs per patient per day, and pharmacies use number of prescriptions filled. As a result the buyer may ask that as of the sale date the business must be maintaining a certain level of activity based on those statistics. For example, I recently had a major pharmacy chain acquire a small pharmacy, and the chain required the seller to have filled a certain number of prescriptions the month before the closing or the sale price would be adjusted. The buyer is simply trying to make sure the business he is buying is still operating in the same manner as the business he analyzed when negotiating the sale and has not substantially changed before the sale date.

Earn-outs: If the seller believes the business will grow substantially but the buyer wants the business now they may want to agree on how to increase the sale price over time if the business continues to meet the growth and targets on which both parties agree. This is a great way for the seller to get a higher price than the business is currently worth. However, as a seller you may become frustrated because you lose control over your business and how the buyer works to achieve your goals. My suggestion to the seller is to negotiate an earn-out if it is appropriate, but understand it may not work out for reasons beyond your control. If you can live with those terms, you won't be disappointed. As a seller, you need to understand that the buyer has things about your business he will change to help him make it more profitable for his purposes. That may mean such items as firing people, moving operations to a different location, and more. All these items will have an effect on the business you sold. So, ask for the world but expect nothing.

Lease of facilities: In many cases, the real estate may not be a part of the sale even though the seller owns the real estate. As the seller, you will want to negotiate the terms of the lease of the facilities, how long you lock the buyer in to renting your facility, and who pays the taxes, insurance, and maintenance. Ask yourself what would happen if the buyer moves out and you are left with a vacant building? Make sure you understand the true market value for your particular property if it no longer houses your business before you negotiate this deal.

Passwords, rights to patents, proprietary data, etc: Today there is more emphasis than ever on privacy issues. Your business may have some confidential data, and you may want to document those items and provide them to the buyer at closing. In many cases, that data is in your head because you developed systems and security as you grew the business. Therefore, you may want to spend some time documenting these items. This is critical even if you have no intention of selling today. If you died today, someone would have to step in and run your business until it could be sold. This information is extremely important for someone to be able to step in and run the business without interruption.

Legal issues relating to actions prior to the sale: The buyer may ask you to be liable for anything that went wrong when you owned the business, regardless of when you become aware of the problem. You will want to work with the attorneys to understand your rights and ability to defend these claims and what responsibility you have if the buyer just pays a claim and then comes to you for a refund when you feel there is no basis for the claim.

Arbitration clause: The costs and time it takes to litigate an issue continue to soar. A couple years back a client went out of business but had some litigation going with the potential to recoup some funds. The attorney agreed to take the case on a contingency, but the client had to pay the out-of-pocket costs until the case was settled. The deposition and out-of-pocket costs were over $100,000 the first year on that case. The buyer and the seller may want to discuss whether they want to consider binding arbitration for any future disagreements as opposed to going to court. This is something that should be discussed with your legal counsel.

Non-compete clause: The buyer may want some assurance when buying your business that you don't intend to start a competing business. The key here is to negotiate something that is reasonable for what you are selling. The seller will want to make sure he can still make a living if he chooses to work. Therefore, you may want to consider things like restrictions for a certain geographic area and/or a certain time period. You may also want to ask legal counsel what has been held as reasonable for your region or industry.

In summary, there are lots of details to consider when selling a business, and every one of them has the potential to come back and haunt you. Therefore, make sure you understand your buyer. The best of all worlds is a cash deal, where you are paid in full and have no responsibility or worry after the sale. In reality, that probably won't happen, so be prepared to negotiate how your business will transition and who will take what financial risks during that time period.

Once there is an adjustment to the sale price for the above items, there is the decision as to how the money is paid. In some cases, a part of the sale price is held in escrow until items are resolved. In other cases, the buyer will make a partial payment in cash at closing and finance the remaining portion. When that happens, the financed portion may be adjusted for any of the changes listed above when the actual adjustment can be calculated. Both parties will want to insure they have plans for how to remedy any adjustments to the sales.

Once you negotiate the sale and sign the documents, it is time to begin to plan the steps to transition your business to the new owners and minimize any losses in that process. The first thing to consider is the customers, and the next chapter covers this issue.

Chapter 34

Transitioning Customers and Employees through the Sale

By Bert Doerhoff, CPA

Without customers there are no profits, and without profits there is nothing to sell. Without employees, there is no one to run the business operations. That is why it is so important to put a plan in place to ensure your customers and employees make the transition smoothly when you sell your business.

Transitioning Customers

How you treat your customers in the sale should be no different from how you treat them every day. You should strive to make sure every time your customers have any dealing with your business, they feel special. Think about the businesses you have referred to others in the past. You probably told someone about some business because they did something for you that you didn't expect. They went beyond what you expected for that type of business. That is exceptional customer service, and if you didn't deliver it in your business before the sale, you better figure out how to deliver it in the transition to the new owner.

Example of how to calculate the value of a customer to your business:

Average annual sales to the customer	$10,000
Average number of years you had the customer	10
(Multiply the two to determine the lifetime value of the customer)	$100,000

Now compare that value to the cost of marketing and sales to obtain a new customer and you will see the true value of making the extra effort to retain and transition all your customers.

Here is a list of steps to take to transition your customers:

Identify the largest and most profitable customers. Once you identify them, you will want to spend the most time working to make sure they transition to the new owner. Put together a presentation or handout that explains why the sale is good for this particular customer. Every communication with customers should be handled from their perspective. They are not getting anything out of the sale, so they need to understand how they will be better served after the sale than they are today.

Make joint calls on key customers. Buyer and seller should select the right people to go to these meetings. Nothing works like friendships, so the person your customer trusted most in your company needs to go on a visit along with a member of the buyer management team so the customer can see how important he is and begin to experience the personal chemistry with the new owner.

Gradually transition people in charge of the accounts to the new management team. Customers were happy with the person you had handling their account, so it will take some time to transition to a new person in charge. Lay out a plan for how you will gradually make that change.

Listen. Customers will tell you what they think and what their problems are. When you go out you should listen twice as much as you talk. Then go back and adjust the plan to fit what will best transition the customers.

Send out communications with signatures of buyer and seller on smaller accounts. Everyone will form some opinion of what is going on; it is crucial you get accurate information to your customer base before they start hearing rumors.

Determine how long you and your key people will work with the transition. Also, determine what the compensation for this will be and make sure it is in the contract so that everyone knows what to expect.

The real purpose of all of this is to make the customers feel like they will see no change in what they have come to expect or will see something that is better. If customers see a risk or downside to the sale, they will begin to shop around. That is why it is so important to do all communications through the eyes of the customer. Once you get a plan, step back and ask yourself, "If I were the customer, would this make sense?"

After you have a plan for the customers, you also need a similar plan for your employees.

Transitioning Employees

The employees are the key to the new owner succeeding with the business. That means you need a plan to make sure the key team players stay with the company to make the transition. Customers and employees are kind of like the argument about the chicken and the egg. Without one, you generally won't have the other, so treat them both with equal importance.

In everything you do in business, you should consider your employees as a key part of your success. So when it is time to sell you need to give them proper consideration. Employees generally are not big risk takers, like you were when you started the business. They like the safety of a paycheck and knowing they have a secure job. When there is a question about the paycheck or job security, employees will start to look elsewhere quickly because they can't afford to lose their safety net.

Here is a list of steps to take to transition your employees:

Understand the buyer will make changes. No two people will ever have the same opinions about how to run a business. This is one of the reasons franchises require you to conform to their system, because they know it works every time. In most cases, buyers are not franchisees and they believe they can improve on your business, so there will be changes and egos will be bruised.

Find out if the buyer plans to keep your employees. You can't be honest with your employees if you don't know the plans of the buyer. In some cases the buyer will consolidate your operations into theirs and your staff will be terminated.

Consider ways to retain those who will be terminated until the sale is final. Your business has to operate until you sell, and you need your employees in order to do that. For those employees who will be terminated, you may need to offer a severance bonus if they stay until the sale.

Consider laws on notification. Investigate your state's employee termination notification laws. Make sure you understand the laws in your particular area or you may have to spend part of the sales price for employee termination payments you had not anticipated.

Be fair to employees. These employees helped you get where you are; don't wait too long to notify the employees leaving them feeling that the notice is unfair. Even if they don't lose their job, these people trusted you and they expect to not be the last to know.

Reward key people. You will have certain key people who not only helped you get where you are but also are key to transitioning the business to the new owner. Consider rewarding them based on customer and employee retention in the sale so that they have a reason to want things to work.

Set up a staff meeting with you and the buyer in attendance. If the buyer wants to keep the team in place, you have to transition their trust to the new owner. It took you years to gain the team and their trust, so don't expect everyone to just jump on board. Sit down with the buyer and explain the likes and dislikes of key people. Meet with each of those key people one-on-one before the total staff meeting so that you can address their concerns.

Look at your employment contracts. If you have employment contracts with employees, consult with legal counsel regarding necessary steps to honor those contracts.

When you look at the overall picture, employees are like family, so treat them the way you would want to be treated. Let them know you care, listen to their concerns, and try to address those concerns head-on before others even know about the sale. Earlier in this chapter we mentioned that you need to have written communication to all customers so that they have accurate information rather than rumors. Employees should receive similar documents. People will always have an opinion, and it is much better to have that opinion be based on facts rather than predictions or fears. Therefore, you must be proactive and put a transition plan in place when negotiating the sale.

After you transition your customers, employees, and your entire business to someone else, it is time to transition to life after business. The next section will help you make those changes.

STEP 6:

TRANSITIONING TO LIFE AFTER BUSINESS

Chapter 35

Life after Business: Wealth Management and Investments

By Bert Doerhoff, CPA

How much must you have saved in order to retire? Here is the rule of thumb: for every $100,000 you have saved, you can draw $4,000 per year in retirement income and increase that amount every year for a cost-of-living raise.

After you sell your business, you still have to address the biggest concerns of the average individual. You must be able to answer the following questions:
- Will I have enough money to retire on?
- What should I invest in?
- How can I protect what I have?

Understanding Your Needs

The answers to these issues come under the heading of wealth management. Total wealth management is about so much more than just investments, because the answers are different for every person. One size does not fit all; to formulate a plan, you first need a deep understanding of seven areas:

Values: What do you value about money?
Goals: What are your family, business, and personal goals, and what are your short- and long-range plans?
Relationships: What are your long-range financial obligations to religion, family, pets, schools, etc.?
Assets: Where did they come from and how are they protected?
Advisers: Who are they and what do you like and dislike about them?
Interests: What are your hobbies, how important is health to you, what types of vacations do you enjoy, etc.?
Communication preferences: What works for you when it comes to managing your wealth?

Once you self-evaluate in these seven key areas, you can begin to formulate a wealth management plan that fits your comfort level.

According to studies by CEG Worldwide LLC, a top consulting firm to wealth managers, the affluent have six key concerns:

Wealth preservation: The key here is not to make high stakes risky investments but rather to make smart long-term choices about your finances to protect your hard-earned assets.
Wealth enhancement: Structure your wealth so as to minimize the portion that goes to taxes on an annual basis.
Wealth transfer: Structure your wealth so as to minimize estate tax upon your death and ensure a smooth transition to the individuals and/or charitable causes you wish to support as a part of your legacy.

Wealth protection: Structure your entire wealth so as to protect it from others during your lifetime.

Charitable giving: Ensure you choose the proper methods and proper assets to support charitable causes you want during your lifetime and in the form of your legacy after your death.

Relationship management: One person should oversee the whole plan and act as chief financial officer, using a consultative approach and guiding the various experts needed to implement the plan.

For those who want to do total wealth management on their own, the first step is a good basic understanding of investments. As you become more successful and can attract a top team of advisers, you will want to turn this function over to them. This normally occurs somewhere around $1 million in investable net worth. Successful people generally start off wanting total control of everything, and over time they realize their success will be limited unless they can outsource key tasks to others. Wealth management is one of those unique examples where the discipline the adviser brings to help you make smart long-term decisions about your money can actually save you money and time. As a wealth manager myself, I have found people want that adviser to be competent and caring, to have character and integrity, and to be someone with whom they can connect. Before you trust your life's savings to someone, make sure that person fits these traits or you will soon be looking for another adviser.

Understanding Investments

Assuming you do want to understand something about investing, you need to know that there are no guarantees in investing, but there are certainly ways to stack the odds in your favor. Based on my experience as a wealth adviser, here is a basic summary.

Inflation and CDs will generally deliver approximately the same return over time. Therefore, as your cost of living grows with inflation, you will not have enough additional income to maintain your standard of living if you invest only in CDs and other types of fixed-income investments. People will not invest in riskier items unless they expect to make a higher return. Therefore, what is most important to protecting your hard-earned savings is understanding how to minimize that risk and still get the highest return for the dollars you invest.

Markets are efficient. Every stock on the market is constantly priced at the market value, as determined by the price a willing buyer and willing seller agree is fair. In this age of increasing speed in technology, the pricing of stocks continues to be more efficient. Research has shown in the fixed-income market that the major adjustment in prices related to new information lasts about forty seconds. Similar research has shown that in the equity markets when there are quarterly earnings announcements after trading hours the majority of price response in the stock price is realized during the opening trade the next day. With millions of people monitoring every aspect of the stock market and the public information that could affect the market, how could we possibly think we are smarter than everyone and always know the next winners and losers?

Risk and reward are related. Over time riskier assets provide higher expected returns as compensation to investors for taking those greater risks. Why would anyone invest in a smaller company they have never heard of if they could make the same amount of money investing in a big company like Coca-Cola or Walmart®? For example, over the long term from 1927 to 2005, the S&P 500 Index (the 500 biggest companies on the market) had a 10.34 percent annualized compound return and the U.S. small companies had an 11.96 percent annualized compound return. That means those people who only invest in big companies gave up 1.62 percent of what they could have made had they invested in small companies. There will always be short periods of time where big companies give a higher return than small companies, but over the long term small outperforms big.

Don't follow the herd. Invest in value over growth stocks. To understand the difference between value and growth stocks, let's take a company everyone has heard of: Google. When Google first came on the market, the stock was selling for $100 per share, and it soon rose to $400 per share. Google was the same company, but all of a sudden people were willing to pay more for the stock. When stock price on the open market is valued high compared to what the company books show as stockholder equity, then the stock is considered a growth stock. A value company is just the opposite of growth. The stock price on the open market is low compared to what the stockholder equity shows. An example of a value stock would be General Motors Company (GMC) and Chrysler® just before the auto bailout. Their stock prices dropped very low even though the company did not change. We always want to be a part of a winner, and that thinking produces a chase-the-herd mentality, which means we want to buy what everyone likes. However, over time it has made more sense to buy the companies that are out of favor (value stocks). In reviewing historical stock prices I have found that the value segment of the market outperformed the growth segment by somewhere between 2 and 5 percent, depending on the size of company and whether you invested in U.S. or international stocks.

Diversification is key. The cost of limiting your investment portfolio to a small number of investments affects your returns. The goal in diversification is to invest in asset classes that rarely move in the same direction at the same time. You might ask why anyone would want to invest in anything other than the hottest asset class at any time. If you could predict the hottest asset class, that idea would make a lot of sense. The key to diversification is to know how much to invest in each segment (large, small, growth, value, international, U.S., etc.) so as to get consistent market returns and minimize risk in up and down markets. A lot of people invest in several mutual funds and think they are diversified, but if you look at the stocks those funds are each invested in, oftentimes they are invested in many of the same companies and asset classes. That type of diversification is a waste of time. If you add the stocks listed on the various publicly traded stock exchanges around the world there appear to be approximately 25,000 different stocks. Most of the mutual funds I have reviewed seem to invest in around 500 of those stocks, and many of the funds own the same stocks. In order to diversify, you need to find funds that spread across a market segment (index funds) and find separate funds that invest in different market segments so as to minimize overlap in your portfolio. Over time, adding multiple asset classes to your portfolio can add an additional 2 percent to your average annual return.

Taxes are the single biggest cost in any investment approach. There are two key issues that cause taxes to reduce returns. First, from time to time Congress has given incentives for people to invest by allowing them to pay a lower capital gains tax on earnings from investing in the market that are held for over one year. Second, you need to understand that once you pay any tax, you have less money left to reinvest. If you buy a stock and hold it, you pay no tax on market gains until you actually sell the stock. However, many mutual fund managers believe they must constantly sell one stock and buy another because they think they know how to time the market. The turnover ratio of a fund or portfolio shows how many times per year the fund manager sells the stocks in the account and buys new stocks. This not only means you may pay tax at a higher than ordinary income tax rate, but it also means you have to pay tax sooner on your market gains and you therefore have less to reinvest because you had to give the IRS part of that gain when the fund manager sold some stock.

According to *The Coffeehouse Investor: How to Build Wealth, Ignore Wall Street, and Get on with Your Life* Bill Schultheis's analysis of data from Morningstar shows that the average managed fund has 87 percent turnover and the average index fund has only 20 percent turnover.[xii] In simple terms, turnover means that the fund manager has bought and sold the stocks held by the fund more often. A turnover of 87 percent means the fund sold 87 percent of the stocks in the fund and bought new stocks. The problem with that is that every time the fund sells a stock, it creates taxable gain or loss for the investor. An index fund generally buys and holds the stocks and will share in the same gain from increase in value of the stocks, but that gain will not be taxable until the stock is sold.

Past performance won't guarantee future performance. Think back over the investments you made and about what your broker showed you. You were probably shown how well that particular fund did over the past one and five-year periods and how much better it did than others in that same period. I hate to break your bubble, but that should warn you that it is probably not the fund to invest in. From 1987 through 2009, there was never one asset class that outperformed the others more than two years in a row. The best asset class one year often is not the best asset class the next year. What is even worse is what happens to an individual investor when he constantly swaps funds to chase yesterday's winners, looking for their hot returns. The investor simply buys the fund that did the best last year and history has shown that no asset class continuously performs above others. Therefore, if you buy into the one that was on top last year, history would tell you that you just purchased the segment that will underperform in the coming years. The net result is the investor that chases yesterday's winners will get a smaller share of the long term market returns.

Understanding How Pension Funds Invest

Nowhere is there more money than in the big pension funds. They have the clout to search historical databases, identify top-performing investment managers, and narrow their choices to the best managers in hopes of outperforming the markets. So what are they doing?

- The following state pension funds use indexing and passive asset class investment funds for their pension

funds: Washington (100 percent), California (85 percent), Kentucky (67 percent), Florida (60 percent), New York (75 percent), Connecticut (84 percent).[xiii]
- Intel® fired all their active money managers in their pension fund.
- Phillip Morris USA Inc. ended the use of active managers for $8 billion in pension plan assets due to poor and inconsistent performance.
- ExxonMobil moved nearly all of $13.2 billion in retirement assets to indexing.

If you aren't following the passive investment approach described in this chapter, please ask yourself what it is that you and your broker know that these huge pension funds don't know about investing. You need a wealth manager who follows scientific and academic research to help you make smart long-term decisions about your money rather than someone who thinks he can beat the market. The wealth manager you chose should agree to be bound by the fiduciary standard rather than the suitability standard under which brokers operate. With the fiduciary standard the advisor can only offer the investment that is in your best interest. This differs from the suitability standard where the broker can pick from similar investments but choose to recommend the investment that pays the biggest commission to the broker.

It is easy to get bogged down in the details when trying to handle investments yourself. What you really need is a wealth manager to help you make smart long-term decisions about your money and also work with you to minimize taxes, transfer your wealth to others, protect your wealth, and assist you with any charitable causes. You worked hard to grow your business, and now you need to make smart decisions about what to do with the fruits from that business.

Once you get your newfound wealth under control, you need to understand what else will change in your life once you sell the business. The next chapter will assist you with those issues.

Chapter 36

Life after Business: Lifestyle Changes

By Bert Doerhoff, CPA

To say your life changes when you sell a business would be an understatement. We discussed estate and wealth planning needs that occur when you sell, but the biggest adjustment might be the lifestyle changes. If you took our early advice and chose a business you enjoyed, that means you just sold something you enjoyed that was a big part of your life and you might miss it. If you don't adjust quickly, you will soon regret selling your business and you will be miserable. Planning for life after business is no different from planning a business. You need a plan, and you need to constantly refine that plan based on how others have succeeded.

Remember, doing nothing is not a choice. Stress is one of the leading causes of Alzheimer's, and having nothing to do can be one of the most stressful things in life when you are used to always being busy. Think back to all the times you saw someone retire and do nothing. Then think how long it was before that person's health failed. The mind and the body are very similar. If you don't do something to keep them in shape, they both slip away.

Here are some alarming statistics to keep in mind:

Of Americans aged 65 and over, 1 in 8 has Alzheimer's, and nearly half of people aged 85 and older have the disease.

4 percent of the general population will be admitted to a nursing home by age 80. But, for people with Alzheimer's, 75 percent will be admitted to a nursing home by age 80.[xiv]

Things to Do for Yourself

Learn to Relax

What happened to those sixty-hour weeks? Even when you weren't at work, your mind was probably thinking about how you could improve things at work. When you remove something from your life that took forty to sixty hours per week that is a major adjustment. You no longer have to balance work and life together. Now it is just life. Slow down and try to enjoy the simple things, such as nature, savoring your food, and talking with your best friend.

Understand Your Opinion Is No Longer the Final Word

When you went to work, your management team would come to you for solutions to problems and want your approval for various plans. Now no one answers to you. You thought you were important, but think about a bucket of water. You pull your finger out and where is the hole? Just a few ripples and then there is no evidence you were ever there. Don't take this personally, because if you think about it, this is just life. Think of all the people who worked so hard to accomplish things, fought in wars, et cetera, and now they passed on but no one remembers anything about them. This doesn't mean you no longer have value. However, it means in order to be of value to others, you need to expand your horizons.

Make a Bucket List

There is a movie titled *The Bucket List* about two men who are dying and decide to take off and do all the things they always wanted to do before they died (kicked the bucket). They call the list their bucket list. Remember all those things you were going to do someday? Well, this is someday. Make a list and start to check off one item at a time.

Think of Things You Could Do That Don't Require Money

Ideas that come to mind include visiting a museum, exploring a park, going to the farmers' market, visiting the library, cleaning out a closet and donating unused sweaters to those in need, planting flowers, starting seeds, listening to music, rehearsing with a choir, reading poetry, and reading a book about those who overcame challenges.

Things to Do for Others

Take on charitable and volunteer activities. There are so many organizations that need good business skills but just can't pay for them. You can now volunteer your time and have the same feeling of value you had when you ran your business. You can now volunteer for organizations like the Service Corps of Retired Executives (SCORE) run by the Small Business Administration (SBA). Individuals from all areas of expertise volunteer their time advising struggling business owners who can't afford to pay a consultant. There are charitable organizations that need your help badly for every area and interest in life, and you will find there is nothing so rewarding as helping others.

Review your insurance for any changes needed. Now that you are no longer working, you probably don't need disability insurance. However, it may be time to take a second look at long-term care insurance, as nursing home costs and longevity continue to rise.

Make a list of where everything is. This might seem obvious to you, but there are so many things in your life that only you know the when, where, how, and why of. In business you had a backup plan, and you turned that key information over to the new owner when you sold. You need the same backup plan now in case you become incapacitated. Would someone else know where everything is and how to handle it?

I worked with an estate a few years back where a woman who was very well respected passed away. This person had actually met four living presidents in her line of work. When she passed away, her mind had slipped and the administrator of her estate found CDs in trash bags ready to go out with the garbage. Worse yet, there were two safe deposit box keys that they never found a safe deposit box or bank to match with. You should organize your records so that if someone had to come in and take over today they would be comfortable knowing they had everything under control and would know how you wanted things handled.

Adjusting to life after business might take some time, but those who adjust don't know how they had time for everything before they sold their business. With some planning you will adjust, and every step in your life can be better than the last. Once you adjust, it is time to think about how you pass your values on to others in life.

Chapter 37

Life after Business: Leaving a Legacy of Values

By Bert Doerhoff, CPA

"Very rarely does wealth survive beyond three generations."
—author observation

You adjusted to life after business but for some strange reason the whole world just does not see things your way. A chapter on transitioning values may seem out of place in a book on business, but who is more qualified to train the leaders of tomorrow than those who succeeded in the past? When we were discussing what should be included in this book, we felt the leaders of today have an obligation to help the leaders of tomorrow.

Moral Values and Government

It is easy to dislike government, but take a minute to look at government and the disadvantaged from a different view. If we all truly cared for others and did our best to help those in need, how much less waste would there be and how much better off would the world be? We have talked a lot in this book about how to create wealth, but with the creation of wealth comes an obligation to share and help others. If we get greedy and fail to meet that obligation, then government has no choice but to step in and help. The end result of government stepping in is inefficiency and greed. People have a need to feel valued and be treated fairly in life. The more we ignore that need, the more we see a breakdown in our social system, and at some point it can also affect the safety of the wealthy as the disadvantaged revolt.

Religious Values

There are lots of different views on religion, but it is hard to talk about values without discussing religion. Over time, I've noticed that religion can be an indicator of better health, larger investment portfolios, and the like. I don't know all the answers to why, but many attribute that to less stress and the ability to put all problems in perspective and turn them over to God. This allows you to make better long-term quality decisions rather than be swayed by the noise put out every day by the media. I am a firm believer that God has a purpose for each of us here on this earth, and when we are called to that purpose we will excel beyond belief.

Sometimes God's purpose for us is not immediately obvious. Tony Melendez was born without any arms. This, however, did not stop him from learning to play the guitar...with his feet. His perseverance over what others may perceive as a limitation, enables him to enrich the world with music where he played for Pope John Paul II when he visited the United States (in 2008 I was blessed to see Tony playing at the Catholic Church near where he lives today). We all face challenges in life which we find hard to explain but my view is God never gave you a challenge you could not handle and as we rise to meet those challenges we all become better people.

Prayers Are Answered

I taught religion to tenth-grade students the last several years, and I always tried to get through to them the meaning of life. One day

I asked the students if anyone had ever prayed for something and gotten it. A girl spoke up and said yes. Her mom had a lifestyle that was not conducive to raising a family, and her grandmother wanted the mother to give up custody of her and her three siblings so they could live with their grandmother and have some stability in their lives. Her grandmother had read somewhere that if you prayed the rosary fifty-three days in a row, the blessed virgin would grant your wishes. The family had all prayed together every day, and on the fifty-third day, her mom called and agreed to give custody of the kids to the grandmother.

I'll never forget that story because it made me think back to how I had often asked for selfish things and didn't seem to get an answer. What I learned was that God answers all our prayers; he just doesn't always give us the answers we want. If you really want what is best for others, the good Lord will help you find the way. Our problem is that we often ask for selfish reasons.

Jesus himself told us "a city set on a mountain cannot be hidden," Matthew 5:14 (New American Bible). You are training the leaders of tomorrow by your every action today. If we plant the seeds of love, we have done our part.

MONEY AND VALUES

I often hear people quote from the Bible and say it is easier for a camel to pass through the eye of a needle than it is for a rich man to go to heaven, Matthew 19:24 (New American Bible). When you think about that passage ask yourself if having money is the problem or if what you do with the money is the problem. You see it takes money to run schools, orphanages, churches, etc. If you look at money as a way to accumulate toys for yourself then this Bible quote may be speaking directly to you. I suggest you spend time making sure you have money to live out your life but at the same time look for ways to use your money to make a difference in the lives of others.

The purpose of this book is not to question the toys anyone owns, because that is between them and a higher power. All I ask is that you really spend some time trying to help others by being a living example of the values you want to see in others. There is a saying in life that you can choose to be the candle or the mirror in life that reflects the candle.

Let Your Actions Do the Talking

Saint Francis of Assisi is credited with saying, "Live your life to spread the faith and if you have to, use words." Think of the real role models in life like Mother Teresa and Pope John Paul II. They led by example and worked to bring peace to the world and help those most in need. They lived their faith and were glad to talk about it if asked to do so, but their actions are what gained them the respect of the world. Pope John Paul II set the ultimate example of leading by example after he healed from the bullet wound he received. How many of us would go into a prison cell without protection to meet and forgive someone who attempted to murder us the way Pope John Paul II did after the assassination attempt that nearly ended his life?

We talked earlier about values and how life can be like pulling your finger from a bucket of water and not being able to find the hole—just a few ripples and then the evidence is gone. As a successful business owner, you want to be able to look back and feel you have made an impact. This chapter goes beyond living your values to how you leave them as a legacy for others to grow and build on.

Teach others. Think of the human mind like the earth. What you plant is what you will reap. Therefore, the key to the future success of others is what you teach today. Learning is a lot like light. We have all experienced the time when we were in the dark and afraid of the unknown, but as the dawn came, our fear went away. Then the bright sun came and we could see some imperfections that were not there at first light. Your job as you accumulate wealth is to help the light to come on for your heirs. Some will get it in an instant, like the flick of a light switch, and for others it may take years. Just don't give up, because the future of the world depends on how successful you are in passing values on to the next generation.

Share knowledge. Ralph Waldo Emerson said it best: "It is impossible to help others without helping yourself." Sharing knowledge with others is just another way for us all to achieve immortality and leave this world a better place than we found it.

Help others. When I say you should help others, I'm not talking about glitzy and glamorous charity fund-raisers. I'm talking about finding a need and setting an example by getting involved to make things better. There is no greater joy in life than that of helping someone in need succeed. Let them have all the credit, and no one should even know or care about your involvement. It is all about helping others and giving. We all have a need for self-accomplishment, but once you have achieved wealth it is your duty to help others succeed and give them the limelight and build their self-esteem. You already had your day in the limelight as you built your wealth. Now it is more important to help others shine and take no credit for yourself. Remember the old saying that it is better to give than to receive.

When we work with wealth management clients, we find that about one-third of them have significant charitable intentions. Once you determine your wealth is enough to support your lifestyle, you might want to begin your charitable giving rather than wait until your death. Think of this example:

If your intention is to support a cause, such as cancer research, wouldn't you want to be able to benefit from that research if cancer touches your life at some point? There are many ways to support charity depending on the size of your donations. Once your charitable intentions reach the million-dollar level, it might make sense to set up your own private foundation to perpetuate certain causes. When you think about whether to give to charity, think of the following three choices and understand you can only pick two of the three:

1. Give to charity.
2. Pass it on to your heirs.
3. Pay estate tax to the government.

Lao Tzu, author of the *Tao Te Ching* wrote:
GO to the people
LIVE among the people
LEARN from them
LOVE them.
START with what they know,
BUILD on what they have.
But of the BEST leaders,
When their TASK is accomplished,
Their WORK is done,
The PEOPLE will remark,
"WE HAVE DONE IT OURSELVES."

Stop talking and listen. Dale Carnegie wrote a book titled *How to Win Friends & Influence People* which should be required reading for everyone. One of the key points he makes is that everyone likes to talk about themselves, and if you are the one doing the talking, you are not learning anything. Silence sometimes can make you look a lot smarter.[xv]

Teach the value of money. Budgeting and investing are two concepts rarely taught in school or at home. How can we expect the leaders of tomorrow to understand financial issues if we never teach them? Spend some time teaching others basic financial skills based on your experience.

Pick a time to discuss wealth with your children. Everyone makes assumptions, and the more you know, the better your decisions are. Wealth is about so much more than just money. Total wealth management involves a deep understanding of your values, goals, relationships, assets, advisers, interests, and communication preferences. If you think back on how much pain you went through as you worked your way through understanding all those things, you will see you actually have an obligation to sit down with your kids and talk with them about what they will inherit and how all these issues relate to their future. I don't think there is a right or a wrong age for having this talk, but at some point in time you should sit down with each child as they mature and show them what you have, what they will inherit, and how the process will work, and then begin coaching them on total wealth management a little bit at a time. Speaking from experience here, I assumed my children knew certain things but found out they had no idea about them when we had this discussion. We all like to keep things confidential so we have a tendency not to share this type of information. However, just ask yourself who can help your kids more, you or someone else who will have to explain what you didn't after you pass on.

Pass on what we learned from our ancestors. Barack Obama had a great quote about legacy in his inauguration speech. When talking about the earlier generations, he said,

> They understood that our power alone cannot protect us, nor does it entitle us to do as we please. Instead, they knew that our power grows through its prudent use. Our security emanates from the justness of our cause; the force of our example; the tempering qualities of humility and restraint. We are the keepers of this legacy.[xvi]

Don't give up. There is a book written by the Simple Truths® organization that explains how at 211 degrees, water is just water, and it takes a lot of energy to get it to that temperature. But at 212 degrees, water turns to steam, and steam has the power to move a locomotive.[xvii] The point is that when we are about to give up, we just need to give that extra little effort and we will break through to the power to move a locomotive.

Don't ever start with the idea that you can quit. It just takes consistently doing the little things in life to make a big difference. You can make a difference in this life and the choice is yours. Your altitude in life is determined by your attitude. Sales trainers often make the statement that if you think you can, you can, and if you think you can't, you can't. Either way you are right. The choice is up to you.

The legacy you leave behind will be totally based on how much time you spend helping others and the difference you make in their lives. The choice is up to you because it is impossible to help others without helping yourself.

The concepts of this chapter can be summarized very simply: Live your life so they don't have to lie at your funeral. Make sure you truly deserve all those good things someone will say at your eulogy.

The End or the Beginning?

This book is all about your dreams and achieving them one small easy step at a time. We started with the planning needed before you go into business and then moved into the steps to efficient operation and long-term business planning. We then discussed how to build a salable business. This final section took you from the sale to life after the sale and passing on a legacy. You now have a solid overview of what steps are needed for you to achieve your dreams.

Now it is up to you to take the advice in these pages and put it into practice in your life. We hope in some small way that the advice in this book will help you achieve your dreams.

Glossary

accounts payable: money that you owe suppliers.

accounts receivable: money that customers owe you.

accrual accounting: accounting system in which expenses and revenue/sales are recorded when incurred and earned.

assets: items of value attached to the business (for example; inventory, company vehicles, cash accounts).

balance sheet: a snapshot of the business assets, liabilities, and equity.

break-even analysis: a report that shows at what point a business meets expenses and begins to generate profit.

business plan: a formal document prepared to describe the business, detail the goals of the business, describe how those goals will be attained, and outline the risk factors that may present problems.

cash basis accounting: accounting system in which expenses and revenue/sales are recorded when received.

cost of goods sold: (Expense) represents the costs of producing goods for sale.

current assets: assets that will be converted to cash within one year, such as cash, short-term investments, accounts receivables, and inventories.

equity: capital (cash or assets) provided by the owner; profits increase equity, and losses and distributions decrease equity.

expenses: costs of producing revenue or sales, or costs of operating a business.

franchise: a business contract in which an independent business (the franchisee) sells or markets the products and/or services of a larger firm (the franchisor). The franchisee often receives training and marketing support from the franchisor and pays a fee for the ongoing support.

gross profit: sales minus cost of goods sold (S − CGS = GP)

income statement (also called profit and loss, or P&L, statement): statement of activity for a period of time, usually one month, multiple months, or a year.

interest: the fee you pay the lender for the loaned amount.

inventory: property held for sale.

liabilities: debts, amounts that you owe (for example, lines of credit, mortgage on business, vehicle loans).

line of credit: an agreement with a credit facility (usually a bank) which allows a business or person to take funds from the bank as needed and repay them according to the line of credit agreement.

net income: income after all expenses are paid.

operating expenses: a summary of expenses to operate a non-manufacturing business.

revenue: results when a company sells services.

sales: results when a company sells products.

secured loan: a loan that has collateral attached, such as real estate or a vehicle.

selling, general, and administrative expenses: costs associated with the management of business other than the cost of goods sold.

unsecured loan: a loan that has no collateral attached, such as credit cards or signature loans.

Further Reading

These are books that we have read and recommend.

Anatomy of a Business Plan: The Step-by-Step Guide to Building a Business and Securing Your Company's Future, 7th Ed. Linda Pinson. Tustin, CA: Out of Your Mind… Into the Marketplace™ Publishing, 2008.

Book Yourself Solid: The Fastest, Easiest, and Most Reliable System for Getting More Clients Than You Can Handle Even if You Hate Marketing and Selling. Michael Port. Hoboken: John Wiley & Sons, Inc., 2006.

Close the Deal: Smart Moves for Selling. Sam Deep and Lyle Sussman with the Sandler Sales Institute. Cambridge: Perseus Books, 1999.

Don't Sweat the Small Stuff and It's All Small Stuff: Simple Ways to Keep the Little Things from Taking over Your Life. Richard Carlson, PhD. New York: Hyperion, 1997.

Endless Referrals: Network Your Everyday Contacts into Sales, 3rd Ed. Bob Burg. Columbus: McGraw-Hill, 2005.

Franchising in Canada: Pros and Cons, 3rd Ed. Michael M. Coltman. Vancouver: International Self-Counsel Press, 1995.

Guerrilla Marketing: Easy and Inexpensive Strategies for Making Big Profits from Your Small Business, 4th Ed. Jay Conrad Levinson with Jeannie Levinson and Amy Levinson. Boston: Haughton Mifflin Company, 2007.

Guerrilla Marketing for Free: 100 No-Cost Tactics to Promote Your Business and Energize Your Profits. Jay Conrad Levinson. Boston: Houghton Mifflin Company, 2003.

Hire the Best, Avoid the Rest. Michael Mercer, Ph.D. New York: AMACOM, 1993

How to Become a Rainmaker: The Rules for Getting and Keeping Customers and Clients. Jeffrey Fox. New York: Hyperion, 2000.

How to Win Friends & Influence People. Dale Carnegie. New York: Simon & Schuster, 2009.

Mr. Shmooze: The Art and Science of Selling Through Relationships. Richard Abraham. Hoboken: John Wiley & Sons, Inc., 2010

Never Eat Alone: And Other Secrets to Success, One Relationship at a time. Keith Ferrazzi and Tahl Raz. New York: Doubleday, 2005.

Purple Cow: Transform Your Business by Being Remarkable. Seth Godin. New York: Portfolio Hardcover, 2009.

Raving Fans: A Revolutionary Approach to Customer Service. Ken Blanchard and Sheldon Bowles. New York: William Morrow, 1993.

Secrets of Great Rainmakers: The Keys to Success and Wealth. Jeffrey J. Fox. New York: Hyperion, 2006.

Successful Business Plan: Secrets and Strategies™, 4th Ed. Rhonda Abrams. Palo Alto: Running 'R' Media™, 2000

The E Myth Revisited: Why Most Small Businesses Don't Work and What to Do About it, 2nd Ed. Michael Gerber. New York: HarperCollins Publishers, Inc., 2001

The Five Dysfunctions of a Team: A Leadership Fable. Patrick Lencioni. San Francisco, CA: Jossey-Bass, 2002.

The Great Game of Business: Unlocking the Power and Profitability of Open-Book Management. Jack Stack with Bo Burlingham. New York: Currency Doubleday Books 1992.

The Likeability Factor: How to Boost Your L-Factor & Achieve Your Life's Dreams. Tim Sanders. New York: Three Rivers Press, 2006.

The One Minute Manager™. Kenneth Blanchard, Ph.D. and Spencer Johnson, MD. New York: William Morrow and Company Inc., 1982.

The Referral of a Lifetime: The Networking System That Produces Bottom-Line Results… Every Day! Tim Templeton with Lynda Rutledge Stephenson. San Francisco: Berrett-Koehler Publishers, 2003.

The Ultimate Gift. Jim Stovall. Colorado Springs: David C. Cook, 2007.

Who Moved My Cheese? An A-Mazing Way to Deal with Change in Your Work and in Your Life. Spencer Johnson. New York: G. P. Putnam's Sons, 2002.

Writing a Convincing Business Plan, 3rd Ed. Arthur DeThomas, Ph.D., and Stephanie Derammalaere, M.B.A. Hauppauge: Barron Educational Series, 2008.

You Can't Teach a Kid to Ride a Bike at a Seminar: The Sandler Sales Institute's 7-Step System for Successful Selling. David H. Sandler and John Hayes. New York: Bay Head Publishing, 1998.

Recommended Websites:

We have found these websites to be of great value to entrepreneurs.

www.6stepstobusiness.com

www.census.gov

www.franchising.com

www.MercerSystems.com

www.SBA.gov

www.SmallBizAccountants.com

www.strategiccoach.com

www.TheDiSCPersonalityTest.com

www.themanager.org

www.Tier2Brokers.com

Bibliography

i   Small Business Administration (SBA) http://www.sba.gov/content/entrepreneurship-you

ii U.S. Census Bureau "Census Bureau's First Release of Comprehensive Franchise Data Shows Franchises Make Up More Than 10 Percent of Employer Businesses," 2007 Economic Census Franchise Report (Sept. 14, 2010) http://www.census.gov/newsroom/releases/archives/economic_census/cb10-141.html

iii Strategic Coach. http://www.strategiccoach.com

iv Business Insight Technologies. http://www.hiringstrategies.com

v   Mercer, Michael. "9 Unique & Amazingly Useful Ways to Evaluate Job Applicants." www.mercersystems.com. http://www.themanager.org/hr/Evalutaion_Job_Applicants.htm

vi Collins, Jim. *Good to Great: Why Some Companies Make the Leap... And Others Don't.* New York: HarperCollins Publishers, 2001.

vii Gallup. http://www.gallup.com/consulting/52/employee-engagement.aspx

viii Kotter, John P., James L. Heskett. *Corporate Culture and Performance*. New York: Free Press, 2011

ix Feltenstein, Tom. *The 10-Minute Marketer's Secret Formulas: A Shortcut to Extraordinary Profits Using Neighborhood Marketing*. New York: Morgan James Publishing, 2009.

x Templeton, Tim, Lynda Rutledge Stephenson. *The Referral of a Lifetime: The Networking System that Produces Bottom-Line Results... Every Day! (The Ken Blanchard Series)*. San Francisco: Berrett-Koehler Publishers, 2003.

xi Tier2Brokers. http://www.Tier2Brokers.com

xii Schultheis, Bill. *Coffeehouse Investor: How to Build Wealth, Ignore Wall Street and Get on with Your Life*. Kirkland WA: Palouse Press, 2005.

xiii Schultheis, *Coffeehouse Investor, 2005*.

xiv Alzheimer's Association®. http://www.alz.org/documents_custom/2011_Facts_Figures_Fact_Sheet.pdf

xv Carnegie, Dale. *How to Win Friends & Influence People*. New York: Simon & Schuster, 2009.

xvi Obama, Barack. http://www.whitehouse.gov/blog/inaugural-address/

xvii Parker, Samuel L. & Mac Anderson. 212: *The Extra Degree*™. Dallas: The WALK THE TALK Company, 2006

CPSIA information can be obtained at www.ICGtesting.com
Printed in the USA
LVOW100633221111
255978LV00002B/1/P